PRAISE
YOUR TOOL KIT I

"Dr. Sheila Robinson's passion for women's development in the work-place shines in her second book, *Your Tool Kit for Success: The Professional Woman's Guide for Advancing to the C-Suite*. Dr. Robinson expertly delivers straightforward evidence-based tools that are animated through original research and courageous C-suite stories of advancement. This book is an essential read for both college graduates to establish career goals, and for professionals to sharpen their career strategies."

DR. MEGAN C. SAGE, ED.D, ACC
Presence-Based® Coaching & Leadership Development

"*Your Tool Kit for Success: The Professional Woman's Guide for Advancing to the C-Suite* is Dr. Sheila Robinson's gift to all women who desire a seat at the C-Level table as she provides critical tools needed to cultivate your development and effectively navigate your organization."

DR. ROSINA L. RACIOPPI, ED.D
President and CEO, WOMEN Unlimited, Inc.

"In her new book *Your Tool Kit for Success: The Professional Woman's Guide for Advancing to the C-Suite,* Dr. Robinson has released another must-read playbook for women of all races, ethnicities, and backgrounds. It has been her life's work to empower, inspire, and impact women and in this toolkit, she does just that by sharing her personal experiences, and drawing on her extensive research. Anyone who reads this work will certainly be set up with success strategies for advancing to the C-Suite."

DR. SHIRLEY DAVIS, PH.D.
CEO and President, SDS Global Enterprises, Inc.

"Dr. Sheila Robinson expressed her passion for advancing women into the C-suite, especially women of color. She was resilient in her doctoral dissertation research and writings in expressing her hypothesis and supporting her research findings to the process. She didn't give up and completed an excellent piece of work to support her passion!"

DR. STEPHEN W. OLIVER, ED.D.
Principal, HRCVision—Leadership, Learning and Human Resources Management Consulting; Adjunct Professor of Human Resources Management, The University of Pennsylvania and The University of Virginia

YOUR TOOL KIT FOR SUCCESS

YOUR TOOL KIT FOR
SUCCESS

The Professional Woman's Guide
for Advancing to the C-Suite

DR. SHEILA A. ROBINSON

DIVERSITY WOMAN MEDIA, LLC
USA

YOUR TOOL KIT FOR SUCCESS
The Professional Woman's Guide for Advancing to the C-Suite

Published by Diversity Woman Media, LLC
1183 University Drive
Suite 105
Burlington, NC 27215
www.DiversityWoman.com

Cover and Interior Design by Imagine! Studios
www.ArtsImagine.com

Cover Photo: iStock.com/Sergey Khakimullin

ISBN: 978-0-9916582-1-3
Library of Congress Control Number: 2017904960

First Printing: April 2017

TABLE OF CONTENTS

Introduction 9

ESSENTIAL TOOL SET #1
Executive Traits 23

ESSENTIAL TOOL SET #2
Preparation 57

ESSENTIAL TOOL SET #3
Building Strategic Relationships 77

ESSENTIAL TOOL SET #4
Creating an Engaging Corporate Culture 101

Conclusion 123

About the Author 129

INTRODUCTION

For the past twelve years, I have dedicated myself to helping women advance in their careers and reach their professional goals. I am a woman, a person of color, and the founder of a thriving magazine and media company targeted at professional women. Much of my work has been to educate women around the country on how to become transformational leaders, and my basic equation for real influence and advancement has remained the same: **knowledge + wisdom = power**. My passion, my mission, and my inspiration in life is to empower women to advance.

MY MISSION

I believe I have a calling to empower women to embrace their potential as successful and powerful leaders. Part of this mission is to help women understand the actions that enable executives to reach the highest level of success in corporate America—reaching the C-Suite. My responsibility as founder of and publisher at Diversity Woman Media is to ensure that women have the essential tools they need to achieve that success. Each issue of our *Diversity Woman* magazine is full of profiles of insightful and inspiring women—of every race, culture, background, and affinity group—who have overcome some of the professional and psychological barriers that we often face, even today. And every year we host a national Business Leadership Conference to engage a diverse group of women in hands-on workshops and lectures where they can learn from other outstanding women who have real vision as executives, entrepreneurs, and thought leaders. The goal of *Diversity Woman* and the conference is to equip women with a valuable tool set to advance in the workplace. Everything is geared toward supercharging the speed of women's advancement.

I'm in a very competitive industry, especially as an entrepreneur, and so I made a very strategic decision in 2012 to go back to school and get the highest level of education: my doctorate. The number one reason I pursued my doctorate was so that I'd be able to provide my clients even more through Diversity Woman Media. My conviction was that the more knowledge I could gain on what was needed for women to advance and gain power, the better I could teach it to others. In 2016, I earned the distinction of Doctor of Education, Chief Learning Officer, from the University of Pennsylvania. It's all about learning management and developing human potential.

Earning my doctorate was an opportunity to advance my mission. First, I knew I was going to be able to help my customers—the diverse group of women who seek out my thought leadership on women's advancement. Second, I knew I'd be able to better myself and the credibility of my business by becoming more marketable and visible. And third, I knew I was going to strategically position myself for the future. I could situate myself for longevity and be able to retire as an expert in my field and even be a college professor. Fundamentally, I have a calling to empower women to advance, and earning a doctoral degree was the next step for me in my own personal advancement.

When I began writing my doctoral dissertation, I chose to research leadership perspectives on advancing women to the C-Suite. I'll speak more of my research soon, but my primary motivation was to gain more knowledge in order to share it as a thought leader. In this book I will share a robust, actionable set of solutions I've learned through both my research and personal experience that will help you advance in your own personal mission. But first we need to understand the nature of the problem we face.

THE PROBLEM OF THE GLASS CEILING

Fortunately, women have been making great strides in the workplace over the past several decades, especially since the women's liberation movement in the 1970s. The number of women in the American workforce has increased dramatically; today approximately 57 percent of women are working, and as of 2012, women represented over half the professional managerial workforce. However, the percentage of women in the C-Suite—those who reach the top-earning status of Executive Officer—remains below 10 percent nationally.[1] The number of women in the C-Suite has been consistently disproportionate to the number of women in the American workforce. This disparity demonstrates an unseen barrier to advancement and is what we know as the "glass ceiling." Women face gender inequality in hiring, pay, promotion, training, and corporate life. American businesses, to their

---

1   Rachel Soares et al., "2012 Catalyst Census: Fortune 500 Women Executive Officers and Top Earners," *Catalyst*, 2012, http://www.catalyst.org/system/files/2012_Catalyst_Census_Fortune_500_Women_Executive_Officers_and_Top_Earners.pdf

detriment, have failed to take full advantage of the skills and abilities of nearly half of their workforce.

These statistics show that the glass ceiling is impermeable even today in corporate America. An in-depth study by Catalyst found that women represented less than 15 percent of senior leadership roles as of 2012.[2] In 2013, less than one-fifth of companies had 25 percent or more female directors, and women held only 16.9 percent of board seats at Fortune 500 companies. Ten percent of companies had no women on their boards, and women of color held only 3.2 percent of board seats.[3] All of these data are problematic, especially given the fact that companies profit from gender diversity at both the board and the executive level.

Having women at the helm is good for everyone. The benefits of women obtaining executive positions have been demonstrated in numerous studies and are widely documented. Those companies with high representation of women board members outperformed those with low representation, and for companies which sustain three or more women serving on the board of directors for at least four or five years, the economic benefits are numerically staggering:

2   Rachel Soares et al., "2013 Catalyst Census: Fortune 500 Women Board Directors," *Catalyst*, 2013, http://www.catalyst.org/system/files/2013_catalyst_census_fortune_500_women_board_director.pdf

3   Soares et al., "2013 Catalyst Census."

an average of 46 percent greater return on equity (ROE), 60 percent greater return on invested capital (ROIC), and 84 percent greater return on sales (ROS).[4] These statistics show that when the brightest minds, male and female, advance to the highest levels in our corporations, it fuels our companies and our economy. It's clear that a failure to advance qualified women will stifle economic and social progress for organizations.

Many companies, especially in recent years, have adopted important initiatives to promote the advancement of women; and many organizations now recognize that those led by women can be as profitable (or more) as those led by men. But unfortunately, in many cases the glass ceiling remains intact. As the women's movement enters its third generation, the low number of women in the C-Suite has become an urgent concern for both women and corporate leaders. Research has identified a complex set of factors involved in women's advancement to the highest levels of success in contemporary corporate settings, including education, experience, technical proficiency, emotional intelligence, leadership styles, and communication skills. Excellence in all of these factors

---

4   Nancy M. Carter and Harvey M. Wagner, "The Bottom Line: Corporate Performance and Women's Representation on Boards (2004–2008)," *Catalyst*, 2011, http://www.catalyst.org/knowledge/bottom-line-corporate-performance-and-womens-representation-boards-20042008

should make a significant difference in a woman's ability to break through the glass ceiling, but still the ceiling persists for the majority of women.

The pipeline of able women ready to join management, boards, and C-level positions is growing continuously, but the funnel for women actually entering the C-Suite remains narrow. The business world has already proven that having women in executive and board positions creates an excellent return on investment (ROI). Yet women don't always step into their power. Why?

MY RESEARCH

My examination of this complex issue of women's advancement in the workplace has been ongoing for much of my career. For twelve years, I've had exposure to an array of incredible women through Diversity Woman Media where I have learned and developed a framework of understanding about what works and what doesn't for women in the workplace. Having basic leadership traits like self-confidence and emotional intelligence, for example, have proven to set a firm foundation for career advancement.

In 2014, I had the honor of publishing my first book, *Lead by Example: An Insiders Look at How to Successfully Lead in Corporate America and Entrepreneurship*. I wrote that book as a guide for women of all races, cultures and backgrounds to navigating the complex business world while staying authentic to themselves. The book is filled with insightful stories of leadership development from real women, including myself. It's about stepping into your power through my equation of knowledge plus wisdom. All of the stories and lessons included in *Lead by Example* are based on my years of experience, research, and coverage of truly strong female leaders. What I found in writing the book was that women have been able to advance to the C-Suite by busting many of the myths that keep the invisible glass ceiling in place. Myths like men are "inherently" more powerful executive leaders than women.

Other myths are self-generated by women themselves in an attempt to narrate the missteps they've taken. Excuses are myths. Women who actually learn from their failures and setbacks rather than make excuses for them are more likely to get ahead. In the Winter 2016 issue of *Diversity Woman*, we featured an article titled "Failure to Launch," where we highlighted some of these self-limiting myths women believe. "Women, more so than men, are highly scrutinized in their climb up the corporate ladder, especially because so few of us have made it to the top." The article continues, "Failure . . . is just one step on the road to the right solution."[5]

Over the past few years, I've continued my journey to research the visible and invisible forces that create barriers to the C-Suite, for women as well as for men. And this year, as I mentioned, I earned my doctorate degree. The research for my doctoral dissertation included personal interviews with executives who have already reached the C-level. I wanted to better understand their perspectives on leadership and map their path to bridging the gender gap. I believe that one way of increasing the likelihood of more women reaching the C-Suite is to demystify the chief officer trajectory by soliciting the advice and personal experiences of actual C-Suiters.

My goal in these interviews was to understand the dynamic interaction of elements that led these executives to their seat, and also how these elements contribute to their success on a daily basis within their role of responsibility. The background and experience of these executives was varied, but their perception of the skills, behaviors, and the cultural ecosystem required to get to the C-Suite were consistent across gender, ethnicity, and age group. The results point to a complex, nuanced, dynamic set of factors that drive women forward in their pursuit of the C-Suite. These include both

---

5   Ellen Lee, "Failure to Launch," *Diversity Woman*, Winter 2016, 29.

stated criteria, like education and mentorship, and unstated criteria, like passion and personality.

The aim of all of my research over the years has been to discover how to accelerate the advancement of women, and perhaps discover a neglected or hidden factor that would lead to a breakthrough.

MY FINDINGS

Through my years of research, as well as through my experiences as publisher of *Diversity Woman*, I have become a thought leader on women's advancement. And I have cultivated a set of findings that offer an empowering promise: women can identify the tools they need to accomplish their C-Suite goals and can actively pursue and cultivate these assets in a way that offers success in both life and career. In this book, I have that new set of refined tools to share with you.

WOMEN'S TOOL KIT

Like a doctor, a carpenter, or an artist, a woman in pursuit of the C-Suite needs a briefcase full of precision tools to do her work. Each instrument is used for a particular task to achieve a specific outcome; and all are used together to create a masterpiece. That box of tools includes the following four sets of individual tools: **Executive Traits, Preparation, Building Strategic Relationships, and Creating an Engaging Organizational Culture.**

Each of these tool sets do not and cannot stand alone. Instead they are interrelated and interdependent on each other. There is no one single magic bullet that will pierce the glass ceiling and make for a successful journey to the C-Suite, but a combination of all of these elements is what helps women succeed at the corporate level.

You may be a woman who is reluctant to even try advancing to higher corporate levels because of negative perceptions of yourself or your peers. The information I will present in this book can empower you to prepare yourself, build relationships, increase your own self-confidence, and develop many other personal qualities in ways that will significantly increase your potential for advancement. I want you to find inspiration in this book about how you can be passionate and confident about both your career and family, how to go after what you want, and stand firm by your goals. This book provides a clearer picture of the challenges and opportunities involved in helping women reach their highest goals.

My heart's desire is that you will read this book and understand exactly what equipment you need in your tool box. There is a problem with women's advancement in corporate America today, but my focus is on solutions. In this book I'll provide you with a holistic set of solutions that will empower you to develop both the professional and personal characteristics necessary for success. I hope you will understand which tools fit you best and apply that understanding to your own life. The results can be transformational for women, as well as for the businesses that will benefit from their presence at the top level of decision-making. But these elements do not work in isolation. They work as a comprehensive set of tools that draft the narrative of advancement to the C-Suite.

Use the tools in this book to propel your own career to new heights. Learn from my research, and from the successes and pitfalls I will share. So much of the current culture and conversation tends to concentrate on the negative or what is "wrong" with women's experiences in the corporate setting. The goal of this book is to make an important contribution to women by pointing out the positive things happening in the advancement of women to the C-Suite. The women who have made it to the C-Suite certainly encountered many of those barriers, like gender bias, but they chose not to see them as negatives but rather as fact-of-life challenges to work through. Because these women cultivated executive traits such as confidence, courage, and assertiveness, and exhibited leadership skills, they were able to reach their goals. So now is the time to take some personal accountability to affect change in your own path to advancement. Instead of focusing on the challenges and obstacles you've faced, let's shift the focus to what you can do right now. I hope you will continue to believe in your own strength and will command these tools with elegant precision. I believe in you, and together we can help each other develop and deploy the tools we need to advance to the C-Suite.

ESSENTIAL TOOL SET #1

EXECUTIVE TRAITS

A recurring theme that has emerged during my years of research and experience is the concept of "executive presence." It's a concept that is frequently referenced and it refers to a wide variety of personal qualities that are often observable, but not easily quantifiable. Executive presence is the holistic set of traits a leader possesses to achieve the greatest level of influence and results. It involves self-empowerment. It involves internal motivation and optimism. It involves poise under pressure.

A number of notable traits that successful executives possess came up again and again in my research as being vital for gaining access to the C-Suite: *Confidence, Assertiveness,*

Courage, Passion, Visibility, Leadership, and Emotional Intelligence. Women who display these tacit behaviors are thought to have the "it" factor. Determining whether a woman has executive traits is a complex concept, full of unspoken assumptions, called "unstated criteria," that don't appear on job descriptions or performance reviews. But these traits have a strong impact on a woman's ability to advance.

Oftentimes there are gender-based differences in leadership style that lead to a biased view of executive presence for women. Historically, women have naturally demonstrated traits that are more relationship-oriented, trustworthy, risk averse, altruistic, and collaborative. Men have often been identified as more task-oriented, transactional, competitive, aggressive, and less cautious with decision-making.[1] These are traits that are often socialized early in both girls and boys from childhood and adolescence.[2] Since executive leadership still consists mostly of men today, the male-dominant style is the presumptive approach for getting to the C-Suite. But research and experience demonstrates that men and women leaders alike exhibit both positional power and a relational

---

1   Rosabeth Moss Kanter, "What if Lehman Brothers had been Lehman Sisters?" *Harvard Business Review*, October 25, 2010, https://hbr.org/2010/10/what-if-lehman-brothers-had-be

2   Deborah Tannen, "The Power of Talk: Who Gets Heard and Why," *Harvard Business Review*, September–October 1995, https://hbr.org/1995/09/the-power-of-talk-who-gets-heard-and-why

emphasis, and traits from both sides of the spectrum are necessary to advance to the top.

Researchers Francesca Gino and Alison Wood Brooks at Harvard Business School conducted a study of 4,000 people, and their research found compelling differences between men's and women's motivation for promotion to higher-level jobs. "It's not that women are less ambitious. Instead, women's ambitions may be different from men's . . . Women may be motivated to pursue positions that foster strong relationships rather than power over others."[3] For years, men have defined ambition as a pure power play, but women are redefining advancement as a blend of power through relationships, position, and personal life goals. The terms and requirements of executive advancement are changing.

Some forward-thinking companies like McDonald's are creating internal executive development programs to solidify skills like emotional intelligence and the building of an executive presence to help their people rise to the top with these critical skills. In the Fall 2012 issue of *Diversity Woman*, Debbie Ballard mentioned a program, called Leadership at McDonald's, as a key component that helped her gain the support she needed within the organization to advance to

---

3   Katherine Griffin, "Explaining Gender Differences at the Top," *Diversity Woman*, Winter 2016, 13.

the position of Vice President, Global Shared Services.[4] But without the assistance of these types of internal development programs, how are women supposed to acquire the executive traits that put them on par with men? How can women cultivate behaviors that are vaguely defined and often based fully on perception rather than performance? First, we women need to understand that each trait is like a tool in our tool box. We must know what the tool looks like, how it is used by professionals and experts, and then pick up that tool and practice, practice, practice!

CONFIDENCE

Possibly the most vital element of executive success is confidence. Confidence is both an inner quality and a behavioral style required for leadership. It's a trait cited over and over again as being the foundation of leadership, especially leadership that inspires others to follow. It is recognized as a fundamental tool both by those who have already made it to the C-Suite and those describing the inherent nature of C-level executives with whom they interact. I challenge you to find a CEO or CFO who is not confident—confident in

---

4   Jenny Mero, "Women Ascendant: DW's 100 Best Companies for Leadership Development for Women," *Diversity Woman,* Fall 2012, 45.

him/herself, confident in his/her team, and confident in the mission of his/her organization. In the Summer 2015 issue of *Diversity Woman*, my "Publisher's Page" is entitled "The Power of Confidence," and it all starts with believing in your self-worth.[5] Unfortunately, so many girls develop instincts early on to defer to others for answers and focus on other people's happiness ahead of their own. But we need to direct the focus to ourselves and assign ourselves the same level of worth as we do others. We do our young girls a disservice by teaching them deference over confidence. This leads them down the well-worn road of under-appreciation, under-pay, and under-promotion that women often travel.

Entrepreneur and columnist Francisco Dao says, "Without confidence, there is no leadership."[6] Dao defines self-confidence as "the fundamental basis from which leadership grows" and something without which leadership cannot exist. So what exactly is confidence, and how do we get it? I currently lead a workshop for women on just that: how to identify and build confidence. It's an intensive seminar that puts women to the test to challenge their assumptions about

---

5   Sheila Robinson, "The Power of Confidence," *Diversity Woman*, Summer 2015, 7.

6   Francisco Dao, "Without Confidence, There is No Leadership: Self-Confidence is the Fundamental Basis from Which Leadership Grows. Do You Have it?" *Inc.*, March 1, 2008, http://www.inc.com/resources/leadership/articles/20080301/dao.html

themselves and others and to step outside their comfort zone. The goal is to help these women identify ways in which they can be assertive and stand up for what they want and need, all while remaining true to themselves.

Many times the challenge for the women in my seminar, and many women in pursuit of the C-Suite in general, is to recognize what life experiences have influenced their perspective on their own confidence, especially at an early age. In one exercise during the seminar, I ask women to draw a "Confidence Lifeline Map" of the various life events that have influenced their confidence, from childhood through adulthood and their career. It could include things like getting a good grade on a test in school, or getting a bad performance review at a first job. The takeaway is to facilitate an awareness of what builds up an individual's confidence so she can consciously work to increase those types of events in her life. Drawing this "map" is one actionable step you can take now to assess your own level of confidence and what has influenced this quality in you.

An attitude that is destructive to a woman's confidence is not acknowledging her own skill and accomplishments that add true value. A 2015 Women's Leadership Study by KPMG noted that while men will often place too much value in their strengths, women will often undervalue theirs. This difference in standards is described as a "confidence gap."[7] This gap can deter qualified women from seeking advancement. Women's lack of confidence can lead them to underestimate their ability to advance and overestimate the requirements to do so. Women absolutely must believe they are worthy of the success they achieve and be confident in their ability and skill if they are going to advance. Women, and also people of color and members of other non-dominant groups, cannot allow themselves to be diminished by the cultural conversation. Believing that you have the ability to perform allows you to project the stance of a leader: self-confident, powerful, and in control. To build confidence, we must also be able to recognize when we have met or exceeded our expectations and not be afraid to let others know.

One of the greatest confidence builders in my career was in 2010 when I was at a discouraging point in my career, partly because of the challenging industry I am in, and partly just because of the nature of being an entrepreneur. But the people in my life believed in me more than I believed in myself; they supported me, and they gave me the courage to continue and advance in my career. At that time, I had an opportunity to speak with the office of Dr. Maya Angelou.

---

7   "KPMG Women's Leadership Study," *KPMG*, September 23, 2015, https://home.kpmg.com/us/en/home/insights/2015/09/kpmg-women_s-leadership-study.html

Her staff asked me to send copies of my magazine and a letter of request for Dr. Angelou to be on the cover of an issue. Not too long after that, my telephone rang, and when I heard it was Dr. Angelou's office confirming an appointment for me to come to her home and interview her personally for my magazine—that put a fire under me! Different things move people differently, but this moved me in the most major way. Later that year she presented to me at my conference an autographed self-portrait of herself with a note telling me to never stop doing the work that I was doing. I cannot tell you how much confidence that instilled in me and that gives me the strength to keep going with my mission!

The great news is that confidence can be a learned trait. It starts with believing in yourself and projecting that attitude outward. Confidence can be displayed at the same time it's being learned and refined. It requires taking your destiny into your own hands and possessing an internal optimism about yourself, your abilities, and your goals. Self-confidence is something that absolutely needs to be cultivated in girls early on. In the same 2015 KPMG study mentioned previously, over 3,000 women were surveyed about leadership. As expected, confidence emerged as one of the most critical tools for advancing to the C-Suite. But what's striking is that 67 percent of the respondents believed they needed more support building their confidence to feel that they could be a strong leader.[8] This speaks to the importance of having a supportive group early in life, including teachers and mentors. One respondent in the survey stated, "If I learned about leadership and how to be a leader as a child, I think it would have taught me to be more confident in myself and express my opinions without caring about what other people think."[9] Some companies offer coaching and development programs specifically focused on building skills and confidence in women. Seek out the programs available to you, whether it's within your own company or through an outside seminar, like the annual conference we have at Diversity Woman, or through your professional association. Or seek out a mentor who can guide you and lead by example to build your internal confidence. Confidence is self-fulfilling: the more we are built up and supported by our colleagues, the more we exercise that confidence in the workplace, the more confidence we exude as leaders, and the more success we achieve. This is what advances a woman to the C-Suite.

Confidence is not just about inner strength, though. A woman striving for the C-Suite needs not only self-confidence, but confidence as a leader. Corporate America is more complex and global than ever and our modern organizations

---

8   "KPMG Women's Leadership Study", 12.

9   "KPMG Women's Leadership Study", 9.

need a leader who can be decisive and is willing to take educated risks. This is leadership in action. Having confidence means being brave enough to make the tough decisions for the good of the team. Our male counterparts do this without compromising their integrity, and so should we as female executives. When you convey an attitude of confidence, you inspire respect and gain trust. Commanding respect and trust then becomes a self-generating cycle that makes you more confident and powerful. Confidence is an important element for effective communication, finding courage to lead, and being sure of your own skill and ability to lead. Clearly, confidence is made up of a number of interrelated qualities, both tangible and intangible, and female leaders can use this interrelationship of factors to express those qualities effectively in themselves. We women can become confident, effective leaders while being true to ourselves, without compromising our personal values.

ASSERTIVENESS

An executive trait that is intertwined with confidence is assertiveness. It comes down to having an authoritative communication style. But this can often become what Deborah Tannen, academic and researcher on gender difference, refers to as the "double bind" for women.[10] When the female leader speaks assertively, she runs the risk of being interpreted by others as being excessively aggressive; if she is more soft-spoken, she may be interpreted as lacking confidence and/or adequate leadership qualities. There is still a lingering misconception that to make it to the C-Suite, or to be successful in general, a woman has to be "bossy." But this is a myth that has been perpetuated by old tropes based on historically "male" styles of leadership. These are just no longer supported by the research on executives today. These are negative qualities that don't lead to collaboration, regardless of your gender or ethnicity. No longer are companies placing the highest value on the masculine brand of assertiveness. In fact, many organizations today are building a culture of inclusion and are creating programs to help employees develop their executive traits, particularly by increasing their confidence and assertiveness through collaboration. These programs benefit women in particular by helping them take on management positions that have the potential for top-level promotion. There are leadership programs like the one

---

10 Deborah Tannen, *Talking from 9 to 5: Women and Men at Work*, William Morrow Paperbacks, 2001; "The Double-Bind Dilemma for Women in Leadership: Damned if You Do, Doomed if You Don't," *Catalyst*, July 15, 2007, http://www.catalyst.org/system/files/The_Double_Bind_Dilemma_for_Women_in_Leadership_Damned_if_You_Do_Doomed_if_You_Dont.pdf

at McDonald's, and like Hilton Corporation's Worldwide University, created to teach diversity and leadership development through a set of comprehensive courses.[11] Many of these programs are targeted at women and are helping drive change in the organizational culture. These organizations recognize the value of all styles of leadership and assertiveness, and these types of programs are accelerating women's advancement to the C-Suite.

To master the executive trait of assertiveness as women, we have to be both decisive and collaborative; to speak with authority without being domineering. We do have to walk a fine line with assertiveness—we cannot be too assertive as to be perceived as aggressive, or worse, having a chip on our shoulder; but we also cannot be so lacking in assertiveness that we're perceived as weak, unconfident, and not trusted to lead. One simple example of how to show assertiveness that we give in the *Diversity Woman* Summer 2015 issue is to simply modify your language when making requests. Instead of softening a statement such as "Why didn't you hand in that analysis?" you should be more direct and say, "You didn't hand in that analysis."[12] You don't need to apologize or make excuses for others. In the same Summer 2015 issue, we

---

11 Katrina Brown Hunt, "Hotel Check-In," *Diversity Woman*, Spring 2013, 40.

12 Pat Olsen, "Speak Up and Don't Apologize: Learning to be Assertive in the Workplace," *Diversity Woman*, Summer 2015, 17–18.

delved into some personal stories on using assertiveness to get ahead. A stand-out story is from JuE Wong, CEO of skincare brand StriVectin. She admitted that early in her career she was hesitant to speak out to get the attention of others. She said, "Learning to be assertive is counterculture for many of us."[13] Wong had an Asian upbringing where she was taught to "be respectful and let my seniors speak." This culture is common among females, who often will apologize for speaking up, or minimize the importance of what they have to say. Wong learned how to be more assertive by subtly changing her language. Instead of saying, "I think," she'd begin her sentences with, "From my experience . . ." Wong said, "When you start with 'I think,' people may think you're trying to be polite, and polite doesn't cut it in the business world."[14] By being assertive with your language, especially early in your career, you are setting a foundation as a confident leader.

The key is to find a place on the assertiveness scale that fits you best, and fine-tune it with a collaborative mindset. There is a drastic difference between a leader whose goal is to demonstrate power over others and another whose goal is to demonstrate strength as a team leader. As women we need to find our voice that adds value as a leader. It's also

---

13 Hunt, "Hotel Check-In," 40.

14 Olsen, "Speak Up and Don't Apologize," *Diversity Woman*, Summer 2015, 17.

important as women that we never judge another woman's leadership style. A level of confidence and assertiveness that works for you may not work for another woman, and vice versa. Many executives who've already reached the C-Suite did face gender and racial biases, but the difference is that they did not allow these biases to deter them from their goal of advancement. Using their traits of confidence and assertiveness helped them move ahead of their peers. Finding the right level of assertiveness is necessary to get to the C-Suite and is a prerequisite for the self-confidence to get there. As I said, assertiveness goes hand in hand with confidence. Leaders need to be proactive and confident enough to stand up for what they believe is right and wrong. And in today's corporate landscape, assertiveness is seen as a sign of self-confidence and self-respect that is gender neutral.

COURAGE

I've talked a little already about the need to be willing to take risks and being brave enough to stand up and speak up. This is especially true for women from Asian countries like Vietnam, China, and Japan, where women are encouraged to be silent, so that just speaking up takes courage.[15] Many African American women, by contrast, are often very vocal and are taught to speak up. But sometimes in a workplace setting, expressing a strong opinion is seen as too "aggressive." It can be tricky for women of all backgrounds to navigate in a way that's authentic and to speak up and believe in what they have to say. But this is the root of courage as a leader. Courage is important in social situations at work, especially if you hear a colleague or peer make a derogatory or racist comment about someone else. It takes courage to stand up and say, "That's not right." This is how these biases among people are perpetuated. I have a personal example of standing up for what's right early in my career. Once over lunch, I heard a peer make a derogatory comment about another female colleague, and I had the courage to confront that peer directly in front of everyone. I approached the person in a calm tone and explained that I disagreed with what was being said. I said, "We should be lifting each other up instead of bringing each other down, and that's what your comments are doing." I had the courage to stand up for what was right and defend my fellow female colleague, and I gained visibility as a courageous leader among my peers.

---

15 Jackie Krentzman, "He Said What? Bridging the Gender Communication Divide in the Workplace," *Diversity Woman*, Spring 2013, 35.

Oftentimes "courage" is an unspoken trait that is seen in the brave actions of leaders, especially at the C-Suite level. It involves actions like jumping on opportunities even when you're not 100% "ready;" being willing to make decisions, take responsibility, and shoulder obligations; standing up for yourself and what is right even when it's not easy or popular; and being courageous enough to have those tough conversations. In other words, you're not likely to become a chief officer by playing it safe. Courage is a tool that supports the development of confidence. It pushes leaders to act on imperfect and incomplete information. It's about having the gumption to take risks and inspiring others to follow you into the unknown. Being a leader means having the courage to step outside your comfort zone—an action that is required on a daily basis at the executive level. Being courageous really means being visionary, because a courageous leader confidently and assertively takes calculated risks in order to push toward the future of the organization and her employees.

Courage is also a trait that should be supported and developed by executives when it is exhibited by the people they lead. In *Diversity Woman* magazine, we have a regular "Point of View" section from Catalyst, a leading non-profit organization with the mission of expanding opportunities for women and business. In the Summer 2015 issue, we discussed how courage is critical to combating bias and affecting real change. Catalyst's definition of courage is "setting aside personal interest to do what needs to be done for the good of the team and acting on convictions and principles even when it requires risk taking."[16] This means doing things like encouraging team members to move forward with unique ideas that have never been tried before, and even helping that team member craft a compelling argument for it. This means taking on the difficult task of ensuring that good programs, like inclusion policies, are actually enacted and are working as intended. This means getting past the superficial and getting into the meat of programs, projects, and teams and supporting them along the way. Encouraging smart risk taking allows employees to develop a better sense of strategic analysis, and eliminates the fear of failure. Many times the fear of failing holds people back and prevents careers and companies from growth. To advance we must foster courage at every level, embrace uncertainty, and not be afraid to chart new territory together.

---

16 Katherine Giscombe, "Women of Color Need Leaders of Courage," *Diversity Woman*, Summer 2015, 48.

PASSION

Passion in your work and your life is an important personal characteristic necessary for advancing to the C-Suite. Most successful people, from entrepreneurs to executives, will agree that passion provides the drive to reach both the intangible and tangible rewards of success. Passion, in general, is a love for what you do. It's the internal motivation to get up every day and tackle those significant obstacles. It's also the force that energizes others. Passion is gender-neutral, meaning it's a quality expected of both men and women leaders equally. Passion doesn't have to be task-specific, and many C-Suite executives have a broader passion for affecting change or making a difference. In this context it's often defined as "purpose" and is a buzzword that has really taken hold in corporate America recently. Leaders around the country have made a huge impact on their organizations and for people around the world by following their passion and purpose. At Diversity Woman Media, I have had the pleasure of coming in contact with, and even networking and building relationships with, some extraordinary women and men whose passion and purpose is infectious. Passion may be the one executive trait that manifests in a visible form. And my own drive and passion for my business is what elevated me to the level of success I've reached today.

Rewind to the year 2008 where I was in the middle of a very difficult time in my life. In fact, it was the worst time in the twelve-year history of my professional business, as well as one of the worst times in my life personally. The economy was failing that year, and I was in an industry where the internet was taking over as the mainstream media while print was dying. I was also going through a tough divorce and had surprises in my life at every turn. At the time, my business was set up in a small business center, and every day I would see people packing up their offices and shutting down their businesses. I'll never forget the vision of all of those people walking out after closing their businesses. And in my own business, no one was answering the phone when I called them, and no one was calling me. The business leaders and coaches who weren't in my industry were telling me to shut down my print magazine and go on the internet. "Print is dead, Sheila!" But—I have a passion for magazines! I love them! And it was that passion that not only saved my business, but turned it into the successful business it is today. What I did during that time period was seriously rethink my business model. I knew that the internet and digital media had to be a part of the business, but I also knew that wasn't where my passion was. I knew it would be impossible for me to just shut down that portion of my business that I was so passionate about and try to do it another way. I'd rather shut down the whole business and find something new to be passionate about. So once I realized that was not the right move for me, I spent an entire week redesigning my entire business model. I knew that most print publications were going under because the traditional advertising model had such a long life cycle. I came up with an innovative way to cut down the long life cycle so I could get advertising for my publication. I also added live events and gave different legs to my business. The result is that now people don't look at my business as just a print magazine; rather, they look at it as a content provider. My business is a resource and a tool that supports the leadership and advancement of women of all cultures, races, and backgrounds. And it was my passion and love for my business that helped me reinvent it and make it more successful than ever.

Passion is a powerful tool. When we have passion for what we are doing, we are personally invested. We are playing to our strengths. By maintaining a positive attitude and having an internal, purpose-driven focus for what you do, you also gain longevity as a leader. Finding your passion is a quest that has also been nurtured in younger generations. Millennials and the next generation of leaders have been encouraged to explore their passions early in life and research shows that they take as much as seven years longer than previous generations to settle into a career choice instead of just following the "job."[17] This generational shift affects not only the career trajectory of the younger generations, but also the underlying organizational cultures for which they will be future leaders. This, in turn, directly affects the fourth set of tools of my essential tool kit, which we'll get to very soon: **Creating an Engaging Corporate Culture.**

But finding your purpose later in life doesn't have to mean delaying your journey to advancement. Many strong women who have found themselves off course have found the courage to change career paths mid-life and have made huge leaps since. Identifying and acting on their passion mid-career can sometimes energize women to leap ahead and get to the C-Suite even faster. In the Fall 2013 issue of *Diversity Woman*, we highlighted the story of Pamela Barnes. After a twenty-year career in corporate finance, she left to join the Peace Corps at age 48 to follow her passion for women's health. This is a wonderful story of not only following your passion but having the courage to do so . . . two fundamental traits necessary in an executive leader. After her two-year stint in Paraguay delivering family planning assistance to locals, she came back with a better understanding of global women's health and women's inequality overall, as

---

17 Kimberly Olson, "The Generation Game: Understanding the Challenges and Benefits of Today's Unique Multigenerational Workforce," *Diversity Woman*, Summer 2016, 38.

well as hands-on experience in how to make a difference in the lives of women at home and abroad. She is now President and CEO of EngenderHealth, a global women's health organization. When asked how she had the courage to leave her comfortable corporate career for the world of non-profit, Pamela said, "It's important to think about how you can put pieces together and how to network with like-minded people."[18] She acknowledged her passion for women's health and strategically placed herself around people and in places that would get her to the next level. She's now there in the C-Suite of a thriving global non-profit as a passionate and purpose-driven leader in her field. Passion is a critical element to leadership and it can give women an important edge to step into the C-Suite.

VISIBILITY

Early in your career, a great mentor or sponsor can help you gain visibility within your organization or career network. Having powerful role models, mentors, and executive sponsors is critical to women's careers. This a topic I discussed in more detail in my first book, *Lead by Example*,

---

18 Marguerite Rigoglioso, "Engendering Women's Health and Leadership," *Diversity Woman*, Fall 2013, 27–28.

and something I will go into more detail about in this book, in **Essential Tool Set #3: Building Strategic Relationships.** In contrast to the executive traits we have so far discussed, which are focused on developing certain personal characteristics, the trait of visibility is more about what you can do for yourself to be noticed and have your impact felt. Specifically, this means creating exposure for your performance. Are you doing exceptional work that creates value for the company? Do others know about it, and do you stand out? Are you getting noticed by those in power?

In order to increase visibility, you need to have a healthy level of self-promotion without the fear of being labeled as too aggressive. Taking the initiative on projects, especially those that others cannot or do not want to do, can help you gain visibility as a team player and often earn substantial goodwill. Jill Tanner has spent more than two decades with Hewlett Packard and retells some of her experiences in the Spring 2015 issue of *Diversity Magazine*. She recalls gaining sponsors early in her career, but tells a story of an opportunity that she accepted mid-career which changed her course. There was a voluntary opportunity to lead a workforce redeployment effort after a round of layoffs. By accepting this challenge, she had several months of exposure and visibility to areas of the business she would never have had access to otherwise. She stepped into more of an HR role and built relationships with many of the people that were redeployed within the organization. When the assignment was over she was tapped for a corporate marketing role. By volunteering to take on a new challenge within Hewlett Packard, she was able to gain enough visibility and build up enough goodwill to advance her career in a way that might never have happened on a traditional work path.[19]

Your efforts to develop an executive presence will be in vain if others within the organization do not know about your achievements. You have to walk the walk, but also talk the talk. Start out with the tool of visibility by developing strong and effective communication skills, and then using that to effectively communicate your value and worth within the company. Make sure that others, especially those already in a leadership or executive position, are aware of what you're accomplishing and what you have the potential to accomplish still. Become the go-to person on new initiatives. Be well-known within many different networks inside and outside the organization. Know what value you bring to the table, and be confident and assertive in expressing that value to others. Women who have made it to the C-Suite recognized that it's not enough to possess excellent skills—they

---

19 Karen Eisenberg, "Moving Up—Without Moving On," *Diversity Woman*, Spring 2015, 27.

must make those skills known, and become visible to their superiors.

LEADERSHIP

So far I've discussed several tools in a woman's **Executive Traits** tool set including *Confidence, Assertiveness, Courage, Passion, and Visibility.* These are all leadership traits that you can develop and hone to get yourself to the C-Suite. But what IS leadership, exactly? When I was doing my dissertation research, this executive trait stood out as unique compared to the others. Normally when we speak of leadership, we are defining the intangible personal traits like confidence. But what I found striking when I interviewed C-level executives, and have found throughout my career in speaking with and working with leaders, is that a distinct definition of "leadership" has emerged.

Leadership can be defined as the ability to rally and motivate others toward a common goal. Leadership is having responsibility for everyone, not just yourself. Leadership includes honoring the contributions of each person you lead while being mindful of your own personal brand. People define leadership in a variety of ways, but the overarching theme is consistent: leaders are those who know how to achieve their goals and inspire others along the way. If you want to get to the C-Suite, you need to be this type of leader: someone who consistently knows where she is, knows where she wants to go, and knows how to get others to follow her there. Confidence, assertiveness, courage, emotional intelligence, resilience, and vision are all components of leadership, and so are motivation and inspiration in particular.

Leadership also needs to be put in the context of the organizational culture. When you are aspiring to the C-Suite, it's for a particular company with particular values, goals, and operations. You must be mindful of the leadership style that is most valued within the organization and know how you fit into that culture. When I first started working at Dupont, the world's largest global chemical company at that time, I was in an entry-level position in the R&D department. At Dupont, the culture was oriented around safety, safety, safety. Every year each plant location would have a major safety contest, and that meant you had to come up with a speech, a skit, or something else on safety to present before a committee. If you won the safety contest, you would get a plaque and recognition from the plant manager. I knew I wanted to get involved and grow within the company; and I knew that of all the thousands of people in the organization, only ten to fifteen people actually participated in this safety contest. So I decided to take part and I actually placed in the finals. But what I also did was create visibility for myself.

I became recognized as a leader within the organization. Within less than a year, something phenomenal happened. When an opportunity came up for a promotion into the marketing department, it was the plant manager who gave me a recommendation. I had been working hard and was a great employee, but it was because I had shown that I was committed to the organization and the culture of safety, and because I created leadership visibility for myself that I was able to get promoted so quickly and be developed early as a leader. This concept of organizational-level leadership is important, because when you make it to the C-Suite, it will be because of the unique blend of expertise, thought leadership, and executive traits you bring to the table. As a woman, this is especially important because woman and men necessarily experience the world differently.

Leadership involves building, directing, and inspiring a team. This more collaborative, transformational leadership style, different from the top-down command-and-control style common in the past, can provide opportunities that leverage many women's personal strengths. So as a leader, you need to go from the assembly line to the front lines. Get to know the people you lead and collaborate across the organization. Be less of a workhorse and more of a cowgirl leading the herd. You need to be able to inspire your group to follow you through your strategic vision. So how do you know if you have developed the executive trait of leadership? You will find that you are humble; you spend more time building up others and sharing their stories and experiences. You will find that you are a facilitator; you are focused on the good of others on the team and how they can use that for the good of the company. You will find that you have a certain equilibrium; a balance between being firm, fair, and flexible. You will find that people are willing to follow you because you are authentic; people believe in you.

Leadership style is something that has become much less of a male vs. female discussion in recent years, and this is a wonderful improvement for women's advancement to the C-Suite. Organizations are realizing that having the power to motivate others toward a common goal is not at all a male-only quality. Men and women alike have the ability to exercise the tools of confidence, courage, passion, fairness, and flexibility equally. And the growing number of women reaching the C-Suite proves the notion that the collaborative approach is also quite a valuable tool.

EMOTIONAL INTELLIGENCE

Increased emphasis on emotional intelligence is one particular tool that can open up new opportunities for women to validate their valuable qualities that help them advance.

Emotional intelligence is "the subset of social intelligence that involves the ability to monitor one's own and others' feelings and emotions, to discriminate among them and to use this information to guide one's thinking and actions."[20] This quality can be demonstrated through effective communication, teamwork, consensus-building, and other vital leadership qualities involving self-awareness, self-regulation, internal motivation, empathy, and social skills.[21] Emotional intelligence is vital for both your own individual performance and your ability to manage others and build a team effectively. It's the foundation of leadership and executive character. Like leadership, emotional intelligence involves the important dimension of relating to everyone within the organization. It involves empathy. This requires a level of self-awareness and taking a look at your own emotional, mental, physical, and spiritual self. It also requires a corporate culture of openness, where input from others is welcomed and valued, whether it's praise or constructive feedback. This leads to real transformational leadership. Pairing the tool of emotional intelligence with courage and assertiveness in a way that

---

20 Peter Salovey, Marc A. Brackett, and John D. Mayer, *Key Readings on the Mayer and Salovey Model*, National Professional Resources, Inc./ Dude Publishing, 2004.

21 Daniel Goleman, "What Makes a Leader?" *Harvard Business Review*, January 2004, https://hbr.org/2004/01/what-makes-a-leader

cannot be confused with "bossiness" gives you the ability to diffuse disruptive situations.

I had an opportunity to diffuse a challenging situation and flex my emotional intelligence tools a few years ago at my annual conference. At each conference we have a set of honorees who are generally top-ranking celebrity women. We present them with a Mosaic Woman award and they are asked to give a ten-to-fifteen-minute set of remarks to the audience. One year we had a particular actress backstage getting ready to receive her award, but her body language in front of my staff clearly showed that something was wrong. When I approached her, she said that no one told her she needed to speak and she had nothing prepared. She was irate. When you have a situation like this, you need to stay calm to diffuse the situation and not let emotions distract from business. It's important to always keep everything professional, even in such emotionally charged situations. I was in a position to take the conversation somewhere else and explain to her that there was a miscommunication, but that she did have options in the situation. So I said to her, "No, you aren't required to speak to accept the award!" I told her she could go up and accept her award and just say "thank you" or even nothing at all. I told her she could say a few remarks only if she wanted. I immediately diffused the situation by making her feel comfortable with her role in being there. I created a warm, welcoming environment for her and gave her options so she could have some control of the situation. Second, I helped her understand the type of event it was, who the audience was (that she was among family and friends), and that we were all just so delighted and honored to have her there with us. By the time she went on stage, she understood the situation better, we had built a quick level of trust, and she was so at ease with us that she ended up speaking for about twenty-five minutes!

In the back of my mind I knew that I had hundreds of women in the audience there to hear this particular woman speak, and I was concerned about how my attendees would react if this honoree didn't make any remarks at all. But the most important thing in that moment was to identify the miscommunication in a professional way, and then create an atmosphere of trust. The only thing I was concerned about was de-escalating the situation, and making this one person feel comfortable instead of threatened or taken advantage of. Oftentimes, when something is wrong in a business setting, it's because of personal feelings. When someone is feeling that he/she has been wronged or taken advantage of, this is when you as a leader need to use your emotional intelligence to diffuse the situation and build trust. You need to use your emotional intelligence to keep a calm tone and an atmosphere of professionalism.

Having emotional intelligence also means listening. Listen to your internal voice. Listen to others within your team and within your organization. Listen to praise as well as criticism about yourself, your organization, and your people. Developing this listening tool will help you establish a network of advocates who trust and respect you as a leader. And you cannot get to the C-Suite without the highest level of trust and respect. "It's about being a good listener," Cassandra Frangos said in her interview with *Diversity Woman* in the Summer 2014 issue. Cassandra is the head of Global Executive Talent Management at Cisco and has a lot of knowledge about business, psychology, and how to get to the top. She continued, "You pick up so much more when you just listen to people. Listening is one of those underutilized executive skills."[22]

Emotional intelligence isn't just about listening and being compassionate, however. It's about being poised, especially in the midst of challenges. It's keeping calm and cool under pressure, whether that pressure comes from challenges within the organization, or pressure we put on ourselves to "do it all." Alison Gleeson, Cisco's Senior VP of US Commercial Sales said in her Winter 2013 interview with *Diversity Woman,*

---

22 Katrina Brown Hunt, "The Executive Whisperer," *Diversity Woman,* Summer 2014, 21–22.

"We have put this crazy pressure on ourselves and we have to put it in check," when speaking about being a working mom. "Don't sweat the small stuff, or you'll feel like a failure every day."[23] She also suggests outsourcing. Outsource and delegate the non-critical tasks so you can be free to deal with the real issues. Emotional intelligence is the "self-awareness" element of all the executive traits and mastering this trait leads to self-empowerment. Stay calm under pressure, and use delegation as a tool to empower yourself to advance.

Think of emotional intelligence as a tool to show your management ability and character. Sharpening this tool will allow you to be skilled at managing yourself and others. Emotional intelligence, like most other executive traits, is intangible. You won't usually find the requirement of emotional intelligence on a job description for CEO, but it's an unspoken prerequisite for making your way to the executive level. Women need to demonstrate emotional intelligence, as well as the other executive traits I've mentioned, if they want to get to the C-Suite.

---

23 Katherine Brown Hunt, "Power Suit: Alison Gleeson," *Diversity Woman,* Winter 2013, 16–18.

ESSENTIAL TOOL SET #2

PREPARATION

Every woman has a personal narrative—a story—and showcasing these stories of success encourages women to push on. But due to gender bias, both within organizations, and in the media at large, it has been difficult in the past to find stories of women who have successfully navigated to the top. When women do reach the C-Suite of major corporations, like Mary T. Barra at General Motors and Sheryl Sandberg at Facebook, the high level of news coverage received demonstrates that such events are still rare. But this rarity does not imply that women are less competent to lead organizations at the highest level. In fact, the first female American CEO was appointed as far back as 1889. This is an intriguing story and is a huge testimony to the power of women to lead.

In the 1880s, Anna Bissell partnered with her husband Melville Bissell, inventor of the carpet sweeper, to operate their thriving business. In 1889 her husband died and left Anna with the business and four small children to raise all on her own in an era with little access to the technology, resources, knowledge, and education that we have today. But Anna had been involved in management and the innovation process with her husband from the beginning, so after his death she stepped into the role of CEO of the Bissell Company. Anna led as CEO for years and was well known for her familiarity with every facet of the business. She was a vital part of the success of the company as she kept pace with business trends, growth, and increased complexity. To this day, Bissell, Inc. remains a successful, family-owned company, and Anna Bissell is considered one of the most powerful women in business history. These kinds of stories, while they have been rare, are becoming more common as women are breaking through biases and ceilings to reach the chief level. I wanted to better understand how women like Anna Bissell have made it to the highest level, and I believe personal success stories like this are the best way to uncover this information. So the research I conducted for my doctoral dissertation relied heavily on personal stories and feedback from C-level executives who shared their own personal narratives of success.

Through one-on-one interviews these executives explained to me what tools they implemented to affect change in their own careers, and they gave their opinions on what it will take for others following in their footsteps. The goal of my research was to identify some of the specific skills and actions that have helped propel individuals, and especially women, to the top rung of the corporate ladder. I've already mentioned the **Executive Traits** that are the necessary *intangible* tools leaders use to get to the C-Suite. What I further validated through my research is that **Preparation** is the foremost *tangible* factor that builds a foundation for success. Preparation should be the baseline of your own personal narrative for advancement to the C-Suite. Benjamin Franklin said, "failing to prepare is preparing to fail," and almost every executive surveyed subscribes to this idea. But preparation goes beyond education and training. It's a nuanced, multi-layered strategic plan that works in tandem with the bolstering of the development of executive traits such as confidence, assertiveness, and passion.

Preparation starts early, too. Getting ready for workplace leadership starts with our children and young people. We have a responsibility as parents, teachers, and mentors to show our children that they are fully capable of becoming the CEO of a Fortune 1000 company. The pipeline for C-Suite leadership starts with raising expectations for our girls. Then it's our responsibility as adults to be the most prepared candidate every time we seek to advance, and also to be looking for the best candidate in our recruitment efforts, regardless of gender or race. So now let's talk specifics about the set of tools involved with **Preparation**.

LIFE CHOICES

Work-life balance is a real challenge; however, successful female C-Suiters have overcome these challenges through adequate preparation, especially early in their careers. Successful people in general will set comprehensive, clear goals for themselves about both work and life, and then they carry them out. Moreover, they don't experience these pressures as a wholly negative, "zero-sum" game of choice between work and family. Instead, they knew up front what they wanted, and they developed a strategy for achieving it. Successful women set inclusive goals for their whole life, both work and family, and they don't believe they have to sacrifice one for the other. Today's world is increasingly complex and the most successful leaders accept that we are all holistic, well-rounded human beings. It isn't possible to set career goals in isolation of the rest of your life. The life choices you make are highly individualized, and as you make consistent choices on these issues throughout your career, you gain the ability to meet both your personal and business goals.

Of course there is no debate that these life choices can create challenges in your career. There are countless stories noting the difficulty of finding balance between work and home and the life choices that women in particular must make in advancing to the C-Suite. Sometimes these choices are exacerbated by outdated organizational cultures that demand work before life. These can be policies like inflexible work hours, lack of recruitment of women with families, and lack of advancement opportunities for women with commitments divided between the organization and their children. These are called "push" and "pull" factors (choosing between the pull of the job and the push of family commitments or the push from the workplace culture) and these factors lead to gender inequality in the workplace, especially at the top level of organizations where the responsibilities to the organization are even greater.[1] Many families today have dual-earners (two spouses working full time) but in as much as seventy percent of cases, women are still the primary caregivers. We encourage our women to get an education to work and grow their career, but they are still raised to be nurturers and care

---

1   "Turnover and Retention," *Catalyst*, August 12, 2016, http://www.catalyst.
org/knowledge/turnover-and-retention

for their family. In today's modern society, though, the choice doesn't have to be between giving up or sacrificing something in life in order to get ahead. Many executives, both male and female, have been creative in crafting detailed arrangements with their spouses or family members to provide for a balanced lifestyle. During my research, I interviewed a female CEO who shared how she and her husband prepared for their career and family early on. They knew before they were married that they both wanted to be CEOs and also to have children. So before they ever started saving for a house and cars, they started saving for a nanny fund. They both knew they wanted to be CEOs and knew they would need the help of a nanny once their children were born in order to continue on their path to become CEOs. So they each made the preparation early in their marriage through these strategic life choices to create their own work life balance.

In the Fall 2014 issue of *Diversity Woman*, we highlighted the story of Tami Blake and the development process she followed with her career coach Jenn Lin. Lin helped Blake identify her core values (freedom and creativity) and how to navigate through starting a new business while being true to her values and achieving a balanced life. In March 2013, Blake and her sister launched their new company, True Waxology & Skincare, the same month that Blake gave birth to her baby. Tami Blake said it was her support network—her sister, her husband, her family—that was key to her success as an early entrepreneur. She said, "Having coaching with Jenn helped me psychologically prepare for the hard work but also cut myself some slack."[2]

Just like Tami Blake, I also heard the myth that it would be more difficult for me to be a mother once I became a leader and an entrepreneur with more work responsibilities. But it was revealed to me that in reality, it was easier! I was better able to afford additional help if I needed it. I was able to develop a healthy relationship with my daughter because I was confident and happy. I was able to be there and support her when she needed me. When my daughter began participating in competitive cheerleading and had to attend cheer competitions all around the country, I had the flexibility of owning my own business. So I took my laptop, I took my conference calls, and I was able to physically be there at her competitions. It helped my daughter understand that we were "in it" together. We were a team. Because I was a top leader and an entrepreneur, it gave me the flexibility and the capability to be a better parent. Many American organizations today are beginning to allow more flexibility in providing for a balanced lifestyle like this.

---

2   Kimberley Olson, "Flying Coach to First Class: The Strategic Use of a Career Coach Can Take Your Career to New Levels," *Diversity Woman*, Fall 2014, 31, 33–34.

In the Winter 2016 issue of *Diversity Woman*, we feature an article titled "Women of Faith in the Workplace" about the inclusion of religion-based needs in the workplace, particularly for women. Hedieh Fakhriyazdi is a senior manager in global diversity and social responsibility at Weil, Gotshal & Manges LLP, and she says her work directly connects to her faith as a Bahá'í. "My profession . . . it's about the betterment of people and the betterment of organizations and society."[3] She often attends social and networking work functions while still following the strict guidelines of her faith. She says, "As I've gotten older, I feel more confident in the personal decisions I make that relate back to my religious values. That sense of empowerment makes it easier to share why I make certain lifestyle decisions that seem to challenge the status quo."[4]

Many researchers go so far as to joke that there is no such as thing as work-life balance! But I've never had a "balance" problem because I treat my work, my role as a mother, my customers—I treat everyone with the highest level of trust and respect. I develop confident, meaningful relationships with each person in my personal and work life so that when those times arise when I cannot be there, or when there are

---

3   Liz Joslin, "Women of Faith in the Workplace," *Diversity Woman,* Winter 2016, 31.

4   Joslin, "Women of Faith in the Workplace," 32–33.

times when I have to reschedule, it's never an issue. I've made those life choices that prepared my relationships for future challenges. You can use the life choices you make as a tool to prepare yourself for the executive track and set a solid baseline for difficult work-home balance choices in the future. The key to all of these stories is not exactly *what* choices were made, but *how* the individual made and perceived her own decisions. Successful women are confident and assertive in their decision making and do not view the impact of their choices as negative in the long run. Women who are strong leaders are able to compromise, delegate, and be confident in their decisions, especially with regard to "life choices." Incidentally, these are traits that are required in any difficult situation, whether business or personal. And being strategic with your life choices is what will help you advance.

EDUCATION

Most of the tools I've talked about so far in advancing to the C-Suite have been intangible. A very tangible element in your set of **Preparation** tools is education. You can earn a diploma or an advanced degree, you can get certifications, and you can accumulate continuing education credits, as well as pursue other specialized qualifications that are tangible assets that prove your preparedness and set you apart for success. Education in general helps people gain necessary critical thinking and analytical skills, and also business acumen, such as the invaluable ability to read financial statements and make forecasts. Education also helps women in particular gain visibility and attention within an organization and can often give them access to more company and industry opportunities.

I've spoken a few times in this book already about my journey in earning my doctorate degree and the many ways this was a strategically important decision in the advancement of my career. During my dissertation research, every executive I interviewed also stated that education was an important factor in women's advancement to the executive level, and most considered their own advanced degree as foundational to their success. Michael Ford said in the Spring 2013 issue of *Diversity Woman* magazine, when he was with Hilton as the diversity and inclusion chief, "My mother always affirmed that education gives you options in life—and that no one can ever take it away from you."[5] Ford has gone on to have a diverse career cultivating employees' potential, and now brings the power of diversity to the Boeing Company workforce as the vice president, global diversity & inclusion. Ford said, "I know firsthand that education transforms lives

5   "Hotel Check-In," 39.

and empowers all, so that they may witness the power of possibility and the energy of achievement."[6]

Women do still face unconscious and conscious bias, and getting an MBA certainly isn't going to alleviate all of the gender disparity on the road to the C-Suite. Historically we know that on average women are reaching higher education in greater numbers than men, with women accounting for about 60 percent of graduate students.[7] But because of gender inequality and the glass ceiling, women have not advanced to the C-Suite as quickly as their male counterparts or as quickly as their advanced education would suggest. In 2013, only 14.3 percent of Fortune 500 executive officers were women, and only 8.1 percent of those companies' top earners were women.[8] So why do we still believe higher education is critical for women to advance to the C-Suite if the numbers haven't proved true? Well, getting an advanced education shows you're serious about your career path and it increases your visibility. The key importance of education is that it prepares you for success in your chosen industry and equips you with the skills needed for a particular job. This is

---

6   "Hotel Check In," 39.

7   Susan Aud et al., *The Condition of Education 2012*, National Center for Education Statistics, 2012, 96.

8   Soares et al., "2013 Catalyst Census."

also essential for professional careers: lawyers must go to law school and pass the bar exam; doctors must go to medical school and complete a residency before gaining a license. In addition, new skills will be required in our fast-moving global economy, and as the cost of traditional education continues to rise above its perceived value, more viable options are becoming available, like online education. So while deciding to get an MBA can be an important choice in your career and can potentially elevate you to the next level, it's important to carefully evaluate the potential return on investment, including what's required for your particular industry. Are there other options available to become better educated, more well-rounded, and better prepared for your career path? Can you get the same knowledge, skills, and advance to the same level by getting industry certifications or attending online courses instead? Whichever educational path you choose, it's clear that having the right level of educational preparation for your industry and position is critical to advancement for women.

I learned years ago from my mother that education was very important in our household. Our family belief was that the more education you have, the more opportunity you will have. So when my father died, my mother decided that her best strategy to take care of herself and her family was to add to her education. I watched my mom go back and earn her master's degree at the age of fifty. My mother took strategic steps to augment her education at a point that most would consider late in her career. This increased her salary and earning potential, and also helped her plan for her future and retirement. She used education as a strategic tool to advance in a way that made sense for her, and it was very inspiring and motivating to me. And coincidentally, at the age of fifty, I also went back to school to earn my doctorate degree. Women should use education as a tool in unison with all others in the **Preparation** set to advance to the C-Suite.

EARLY CAREER SUCCESS

Early career success is another important tool used in advancing your career to the C-Suite and is a complementary tool to *Education*. High quality performance such as making record sales or bringing in new clients in the earlier stages of your career provides both the experience and the visibility for promotion. In the *Diversity Woman* Summer 2015 issue, Jan Combopiano, senior vice president and research chief officer at Catalyst, emphasizes that success in the workplace starts with being a great performer. "If you can deliver on what you say you can do—and help your team, manager and organization succeed—people will take notice."[9]

Experience and success early in your career is just as important as your educational background and these two preparation tools should be used together. Early success in particular gives you an opportunity to showcase your value within your organization. It demonstrates that you are ready for progressively more responsibility and promotion. It also builds up your resume which attracts new opportunities outside your current organization. The key to the *Early Success* tool is that you really need to utilize it consistently. You should always be working hard and smart in your current position to prove that you have the background and skills necessary to advance. You should also be looking for opportunities to show initiative, like volunteering for high visibility tasks. Remember my story in the *Leadership* section about volunteering for the safety contest at Dupont? It's those kinds of early career choices that can set you apart. You should be setting high level goals for yourself to keep yourself driving forward. The road to the C-Suite is not built overnight. It's built over years of progressive experience and success,

---

9   Karen Eisenberg, "Eight Ways to Advance Your Career and Boost Your Pay," *Diversity Woman*, Summer 2016, 25.

particularly early in your career when the foundation is being laid for your career path.

There were times early in my career where I felt the managers I was working for were giving me way more work than I was getting paid to do. There were times I was sure I was juggling two or three distinct job titles all by myself. And in all honesty, I complained about it and I was bitter, although in hindsight I wish I had embraced it as a learning opportunity. I had so many responsibilities, and I was learning to multi-task and prioritize and even delegate. These challenges prepared me to become the entrepreneur I have become and to grow my business to the place it is today. We need to embrace learning opportunities within our organization, even when they are disguised as challenges, because these experiences are preparing us for advancement later on in our professional life.

People who find themselves successful in their later careers regularly report that it was because of early career success. They made life and education choices that prepared them for the future. Early career wins will also give us insight to our own strengths and passion. Oftentimes when we are just starting out, or even when we are looking to make a big transition to a new role, we don't yet know our own capabilities. We haven't been tested or stretched enough to identify what we're really good at—what we're really passionate about.

If you're at that point in your career where you have the ambition to advance but you don't know what direction to go in, you can use this preparation tool to set some stretch goals and push yourself to get some early wins. Identify your true passion and then develop that tool as part of your **Executive Traits** tool set. And like the other tools in this **Preparation** tool set, early career success is a supplemental asset. Each tool alone will not get you to the C-Suite; rather, they work together, along with your crisp set of executive traits, that will validate your knowledge, experience, preparedness, and ambition to advance in your career and make it to the C-Suite. That includes being confident, assertive, and creating visibility for yourself by making sure your peers and leaders within the organization are aware of your successes and of the value you bring to the company.

BROAD BUSINESS LEARNING

Beyond formal education and training programs, continued learning is critical to advancing to the C-Suite. This learning often involves taking personal initiative to seek out experiences beyond the department or job description. It means being a "student" of the organization and studying all of its moving parts. This process of remaining open and learning new things is vital for advancement in the corporation.

And the broader the business understanding you have, the more prepared you will be to move into the executive suite seat that inherently holds responsibility for all aspects of the business.

Throughout my time at Dupont, I had opportunities to build and use broad business learning to advance tremendously. When I worked on the manufacturing side early in my career, I studied and learned the science behind how our fibers and textiles were made. Fast forward ten years, and I was attending trend presentations given by Dupont scientists to persuade CEOs and senior level executives of partner corporations to use our materials in their clothing products. Later while I was in the Marketing & Communications division, I was given the fascinating opportunity to take the fashion designer Zac Posen through a tour of Dupont's R&D and manufacturing plant in Willmington, Delaware, to help him learn about our lycra and other textiles. I continued to put myself in situations where I could learn about the science of our ingredients and our brands, and that paid off significantly for my last role with the company as Marketing Communications Manager. Having that broad business understanding of the products and services at Dupont positioned me to work with senior level executives and celebrities as I managed the PR and communications teams.

The role of a CEO is not the job of a narrow specialist, but instead requires broad business understanding. Academic qualifications and technical skills such as P&L analysis are valuable and necessary, but are not as important as your executive traits (part of the first set of essential tools) and the ability to remain open, to learn, and to be able to relate to a broad range of people within the corporation in a way that values and leverages their skills. Some executives have noted the benefits of working for small businesses or startups in order to gain broad business learning. By the nature of these companies you will often have a diverse set of responsibilities and experiences and more opportunities to step out of your narrow job description. In these small businesses, everything needs to get done, and there are limited people to do the tasks. Either way, the focus should be on your initiative as a leader to succeed and your ability to work well within the organization, small or large. Without accumulating an understanding of not only your own functional expertise but also how everything interrelates in the organization, you cannot effectively lead. If you want to be able to master the organizational landscape and navigate to the C-Suite, you need to develop your broad business learning tools early and continuously.

Lifelong learning is a trend in America today and the most successful leaders have embraced this as a lifestyle. In

Diversity Woman Winter 2016, we showcase Jo Ann Jenkins, prominent CEO of AARP (American Association of Retired Persons). Jenkins is a lifelong learner. She is always seeking out new areas to learn, explore, and be disruptive. Jenkins took over as CEO of AARP in 2014 at the age of 57, a time when many of her colleagues were preparing for retirement and a period of decline. But Jenkins is energetic, innovative, and unmatched in personal drive. She is reimaging aging, not just for AARP members, but for the American society as a whole, by challenging our ideas and expectations for Americans over 50. She says, "I'm very comfortable with my age. I am a more purposeful person because of the experience and wisdom those years have brought me."[10] Never let your curiosity and thirst for knowledge dissipate. Women like Jenkins who have made it to the executive suite have remained lifelong students—of the business, of the culture, and of the motivations of others and themselves.

---

10 Jackie Krentzman, "Disrupt Aging," *Diversity Woman,* Winter 2016, 41.

ESSENTIAL TOOL SET #3

BUILDING STRATEGIC RELATIONSHIPS

The third set of tools women need to use to advance to the C-Suite involves strong, strategic relationships. These are support systems that can be formal or informal, structured or unstructured. The goal of building up these support systems is to make each relationship a strategic tool to be used for your advancement. Fifteen out of seventeen executive respondents queried during my dissertation research stressed the importance of building informal relationships, and networking in particular. In the 2015 KPMG Women's Leadership Study, 82 percent of women surveyed said that networking relationships with other female leaders helped advance their careers.[1] Two thirds said the most important leadership lessons they learned were from other women, especially through more structured relationships such as mentoring and coaching.[2] This is one area where the modern organization has been adopting programs and strategies to help their women break the glass ceiling, particularly through mentoring, coaching, sponsoring, and training programs. These programs are all related to building a strategic network of relationships as well as creating visibility, which I discussed in the **Executive Traits** section. A Catalyst study from 2003 concluded that the key to the success of these programs was that both men and women needed to be involved in order to promote equal opportunity advancement to the executive office.[3] Female leaders especially should play an active role in advising and mentoring their fellow colleagues.[4] We already know the research is clear that increasing the number of women in positions of power is the only way to achieve true equality in the workplace, and we have

1   "KPMG Women's Leadership Study," 6.

2   "KPMG Women's Leadership Study," 6.

3   Sheila Wellington, Marcia Brumit Kropf, and Paulette R. Gerkovich, "What's Holding Women Back?" *Harvard Business Review,* June 2003, https://hbr.org/2003/06/whats-holding-women-back

4   Wellington et al., "What's Holding Women Back?"

confirmation that the most effective way to achieve equality is for women to help each other to develop their relationship tools and build their support networks to reach their full potential as C-Suite leaders. Women need to view all of these relationships as complementary tools and develop each one independently as well as collectively.

In the Summer 2016 issue of *Diversity Woman*, we shared an article titled "Eight Ways to Advance Your Career and Boost Your Pay." Nearly half of the tips provided by our experts in this one article point to **Building Strategic Relationships,** the essence of the third set of essential tools women need to advance. Some of those tips are as follows:

- **Build your network**—Ann Daly, career and life coach at Women Advance, says, "The single most important piece of advice I can give women is to start building their social capital from the very beginning and never stop."[5]

- **Cultivate sponsors**—"Find out who the power players are in your organization or industry . . . then figure out how to strategically network with them in a way that helps them see your value," says Kristine Perez-Foley,

---

5   "Eight Ways to Advance Your Career and Boost Your Pay," 26.

executive coach and leadership consultant with Korn Ferry Hay Group.[6]

■ **Be strategic**—Perez-Foley goes on to say, "The key to growth, whether in salary or in career progression, is getting those highly visible assignments that are important to the organization."[7]

Perseverance and persistence are critical to building strategic relationships. Many years ago I went to a conference in New York and I heard Dr. Annie McKee speak. Dr. McKee is founder of Teleos Leadership Institute, a global consulting firm, and I was mesmerized by her message. I knew that before the end of the day I had to meet her in person. My plan was to approach her, exchange business cards, and ask her if I could mail her copies of my magazines. All I could think about was getting her to speak at my Business Leadership Conference the next year. I wanted my attendees to experience what I had just experienced during this talented woman's presentation. I did it. I introduced myself, and she agreed to have me send her my magazines. She liked them and soon after we scheduled a time to talk again. When we

---

6   "Eight Ways to Advance Your Career and Boost Your Pay," 26.

7   "Eight Ways to Advance Your Career and Boost Your Pay," 26.

spoke she told me about the current work she was doing writing a textbook—she's a writer for university-level textbooks for Pearson Books, a major educational publisher. She said she would like to include me in one of the chapters on entrepreneurship. She thought the students could learn from my story. I was thrilled!

I've always been told that networking, mentoring, and sponsorship, works as a two-way street. You've got to be willing to give in order to receive. Any time you walk into a networking opportunity to receive and not give, the outcome will not be as successful. I recommend never building and utilizing a relationship without the intent of giving back. I saw this connection with Dr. McKee as a perfect two-way opportunity. She wanted to interview me for her textbook, and then I could ask her to speak at my conference! So at the end of our first interview for the book piece, I asked her the question. "Can you speak at my conference? I'd love to have you! Your message is so inspiring . . ." But Dr. McKee replied, "I'm so sorry Sheila, I'm just incredibly swamped." Okay, I was disappointed, but I understood. After some time passed she sent me a finished copy of the book. I followed up with her again around a year later about speaking at my conference, but again she was swamped. Another two or three years passed and it was time for her to revise and update the textbook. She told me that the chapter I was featured in was received really well by the students and she wanted to interview me again and use my picture. This was all great exposure for me and very exciting, but I still really wanted her to speak at my conference! But I knew she was still going to be too busy, so I tried to think of some other way I could ask her for her support and continue to build a reciprocal relationship. I knew Dr. McKee was a brilliant, well-connected woman, so I decided to tap into that by asking for her advice and opinion. After that interview for the textbook update, I told her that I'd been thinking of going back to school to get my PhD. I told her about the top three schools I had in mind and I just wanted to get her feedback. She gave me her thoughtful opinion on each, then made a conclusion: "If I were you, I'd consider the Chief Learning Officer Doctorate program at the University of Pennsylvania." At the time, she was on the board of directors and was very familiar with the program offering. She thought it would be an incredible opportunity and a great fit for me, and she graciously offered to write me a letter of recommendation.

During my second year in the program, the director left. The position was offered to Dr. McKee, and she accepted. She is now the director of GSE's PennCLO Executive Doctoral Program. What a coincidence! She was the person who hooded me when I graduated in May 2016 and it was a tear-jerker moment. To top it off, she did finally end up speaking at my conference, before I graduated. It just took about six years with lots of twists and turns in our relationship before it happened. A key point here is that you can never give up on professional relationships. You cannot always see ahead as to why a relationship is strategic at the time you're building it. Building a strategic relationship is not about getting an immediate result. It's about enjoying knowing someone with talent and being able to say that you are a part of her network. It's about not utilizing a resource that powerful for anything other than gaining knowledge, and just letting the relationship develop over time. The value of relationship-building is immeasurable because it serves as the foundation for a long, successful career, particularly for one on the C-Suite track. It's your responsibility as a woman to nurture your connections. Take initiative and fully embrace these programs and personal relationships. Apply your emotional intelligence and confidence as you build strong relationships to help you become more successful on the job and lay the groundwork for your executive track.

BUILDING A NETWORK

I consider networking to be one of the most powerful tools we have for advancement. Networking encompasses not only our work life but also our everyday life. It includes cultivating mentors as well as mentees, staying connected to peers and associates, joining professional groups, and attending conferences. It also means connecting with people in your community and neighborhood, and joining groups like Toastmasters or the board of a local non-profit. So many opportunities arise through keeping our eyes and ears open and talking to everybody who crosses our path.

Not everyone understands the true value of networking. It doesn't just mean passing out business cards or keeping in touch with someone you met at an event. True networking harnesses the power of real, strategic professional relationships. When I decided that I wanted to get into magazine publishing, I didn't actually know very much about the industry, so I had to start by researching and teaching myself. I wanted to learn everything I could to become the best I could in this new-to-me industry. I searched online for any information relating to magazine publishing, and I looked into trade associations. It turns out one of the most valuable elements of building a network is to join a trade association in the industry you're affiliated with. During my research I came across something that referenced the "National Association for Women in Periodical Publishing." I nearly lost my mind! It was clear I had found *exactly* what I was looking for and it was targeted directly at me. I learned it was a trade association for women in that field, and they were based in

San Francisco, CA. The first thing that came to my mind was, "I'd love to visit San Francisco! What do I need to do to get into this organization?" I never thought, "Oh, that's across the country. It's not going to work out." I knew this was my golden opportunity to network in my new field. I immediately sent off my introductory email and application to join, and within no time I had a response. I received a request to be on a conference call with some of the members, and during that call they were delighted to have the interest of someone who could bring regional diversity to their group. Most of their members were out of New York or California, so they were excited to have a member from the southeast in North Carolina.

I was accepted, and within less than a year of membership, I was asked to become a board member so that I could help recruit more women members from my region. As a result of my board membership, I was qualified to apply for a scholarship to Stanford University's Magazine Publishing Program, one of the top in the world at the time. I was nominated for that scholarship, won it, and I can honestly say my business is where it is today as a direct result of receiving that scholarship and attending that program. It's where I met the right people who taught me everything and helped me build my strategic network in magazine publishing. I was in classes with the editor of *Glamour* magazine, Cynthia Leive. I had lunch with Richard Stolley, the founding editor of *People Magazine*, and one of the most prominent people in the history of journalism and magazine publishing, especially for his work with *Time* and *Life* magazines. I met with Keith Clinkscales, the man who helped bring *Vibe Magazine* to life, one of the most influential magazines in pop culture history. It's through that network of relationships that I was introduced to two people who became my editor and creative director, and who are still based in San Francisco today. I learned so much. The high caliber of people I met through my trade organization and the program at Stanford, who became part of my professional network, gave me a tremendous boost in my professional career efforts.

That is the power of a network. It started with basic research into trade organizations in my industry and led to a huge, strategic, and diverse network. I hope this also shows you a simple and strategic way to start building a network beyond just collecting a business card at a luncheon. A good network is a powerful web in your tool kit that you can use to extend your reach and make connections you never thought possible.

MENTORING

Mentoring is an interpersonal relationship that can be described as a "learning partnership." Your mentor is your tool for learning what it takes to advance. Your mentoring relationship should focus on both career advancement and personal growth, and is a great supplement to other tools, like education and networking. Just like all the tools in your tool kit, effective mentoring requires consistent interaction and reciprocity: once you've mastered the tools you've received as a mentee, it's time to pass those tools on and become a mentor yourself. Typically, formal mentor relationships last six months to a year, but informal relationships can continue for years.

Mentoring programs within an organization are beneficial because they can build loyalty to the organization itself, create a more supportive environment, and have a larger effect on internal career development. This is partly because the mentor can introduce you into social and professional networks that make you more visible within the organization. Other times self-selected mentoring relationships are more effective than more formal, company-initiated relationships. Either way, a mentor can help you gain the confidence you need to advance by helping you learn how to be visible and encouraging you to take risks and see your own potential.

It's your responsibility to establish the kind of mentor relationship that's right for your goals of advancement. You can even use someone as a mentor before you officially ask them formally. When I was still working entry level at Dupont, I identified a young lady in the New York office that I really admired and wanted to be my mentor. I was based in North Carolina, so I took every opportunity offered to be in the New York office so I could observe her. I would inquire about the projects she was working on, and I also told her of my interest in getting into her marketing world. Over a period of a few years I got to know her, she got to know me and my interests, and I made myself visible to her and her team. By the time I was really in a position to ask for a mentor, I asked her and she said yes. But during the years leading up to that time, I was learning from her and building an informal mentorship relationship. Fast forward a few years later, I received a series of promotions and eventually ended up working directly under her on the Global Marketing Textiles team.

Another person I consider a mentor and advisor is Dr. Johnnetta Cole. When she was President of Bennett College for Women, a volunteer opportunity was extended to me to support her initiatives. I was introduced to someone in her organization who knew I had a career magazine and this person wanted me to write about the work being done at the college. Once again, networking and strategic relationships involves a two-way street. This was my opportunity to give back to someone who I admired greatly. And volunteering to support Bennett College's initiatives was also a natural fit, being a college for diverse women. Over the years of volunteering and getting to work with Dr. Cole on several projects, we developed a beautiful relationship. She became one of my biggest supporters as I worked towards my doctorate degree, and she also became a big supporter and advocate of the work I do, with my magazine and live events (attending and speaking). Now I am on newsstands and in bookstores nationwide, and we are featuring Dr. Cole on the cover of the *Diversity Woman* Winter 2017 issue in honor of her retirement. This is what I mean about a two-way street. You should always have in mind how you can give back to the mentors and people who support you on your journey toward advancement.

COACHING

Coaching is another interpersonal relationship that focuses on practical preparation for future advancement, and is distinguished from in-house training that focuses on mastering present skills. Coaching involves learning, development, behavioral change, performance, leadership, and organizational commitment.[8] Coaching is often provided in-house, whether as a coaching relationship between a manager and her team members, or through professional coaching programs, like ones provided by HR departments or through retired CEOs. For example, Cassandra Frangos, whom I mentioned under the *Emotional Intelligence* section, serves as a coach and "therapist" to the highest executives at Cisco who've already reached the top. In her interview with *Diversity Woman*, she said, "As a talent leader, that is the essence of what I do . . . understanding the psychology of leaders, the system around them, and helping them reach their potential and beyond."[9]

Coaching can come in different forms, as, for example, a trusted advisor or career coach that counsels you on whether a job opportunity is the right fit for your skills and career goals. A coach can be someone who is a good listener and helps you identify and sharpen your leadership style and communication style. In the Fall 2015 issue we featured Tameika Pope who does just that. Her passion is personal development and she not only serves as a leader providing coaching and consulting within the U.S. Federal Reserve

---

8   Baek-Kyoo (Brian) Joo, Jerilynn S. Sushko, and Gary N. McLean, "Multiple Faces of Coaching: Manager-as-Coach, Executive Coaching, and Formal Mentoring," *Organization Development Journal*, Spring 2012, 19–35.

9   Hunt, "The Executive Whisperer," 21–22.

System, but she is also an entrepreneur who has launched a series of companies related to human capital development. Her entrepreneurial endeavors include CULTIVATE, a professional human capital development coaching and consulting business; Evolution Partners, a relationship coaching business; and African-American Women's Leadership Network (AAWLN), a non-profit mentoring organization. There is no doubt that Pope is an expert on professional coaching and building strategic relationships and helps executives as well as minority women cultivate their own professional development. When asked how important relationships are to succeeding in the workplace, she replied, "Many times, relationship currency will outweigh performance currency, so it would be wise to invest in building and maintaining strong relationships."[10]

SPONSORING

Sponsoring is a newer tool that is similar to mentoring but includes the dimension of advocacy. A sponsor should be your advocate within the organization. This is probably the most strategic of interpersonal relationships, with

---

10 Tamara E. Holmes, "The Courage to be Herself," *Diversity Woman,* Fall 2015, 22.

the sponsor's expressed goal of actively making you public and visible within the organization. The *Sponsoring* tool is a direct complement to the *Visibility* tool discussed in the **Executive Traits** section. While both mentors and sponsors can provide networking opportunities, sponsors are more likely to make more challenging experiences available and to push their protégé to take more risks, while also providing backup to mitigate the danger of those risks. Organizations can use sponsorship as a talent management strategy by addressing diversity concerns, especially when the program is transparent, strategic, and meeting stated expectations.

A sponsor is generally a senior level professional who naturally has a position of power in the company that can influence advancement. Sponsors provide exposure to their important networks, they contribute to the development of leadership skills, and they help to open up promotion and advancement opportunities. Kristine Perez-Foley, who was first quoted under the Building Strategic Relationships tool, says sponsors are "people with clout who passionately support you and are willing to put their name on the line for you."[11]

Again, you have the ultimate responsibility for getting the most out of your sponsor. Seek them out and approach them

---

11   "Eight Ways to Advance Your Career and Boost Your Pay," 26.

for help when necessary. Also make sure to continue to advance in your current position, do good work, and make sure you have the accomplishments and preparation to support the voice your sponsor provides (see the **Preparation** tools section). Ruchika Tulshyan, author of *The Diversity Advantage: Fixing Gender Inequality in the Workplace*, gives some great insight into the need for and benefits of sponsorship. She explains that while both women and men today often have a mentor, men are 46 percent more likely, on average, to have a sponsor.[12] Part of this is because men are often more comfortable networking outside of professional channels, such as on the golf course or over dinner, while women tend to shy away from this "networking with a purpose." Tulshyan emphasizes the connection between women possessing the executive traits of confidence, assertiveness, courage, and visibility, and successful career advancement. Women, especially those at a high level and with C-Suite potential, really must take strategic action to find sponsors who will advocate for them in the organization and help them gain visibility. Make sure to be direct with your sponsor about your career goals and then back that up with your hard work on the job.

---

12 Ruchika Tulshyan, "Sponsors Help Women," *Diversity Woman*, Summer 2016, 29.

By the way, a sponsor can be a man or a woman within the company. When I was still in my entry level position at Dupont in the manufacturing division, my immediate supervisor, Mr. Bob Seymour, was concerned that I was too content where I was. But he knew how huge the Dupont organization was and could see so much further in terms of future possibilities for me than the actual manufacturing plant I walked into every morning. He encouraged me to consider applying for different positions in other divisions of Dupont. At first I couldn't believe him. I was young and maybe a little naïve. My perspective was that I had a college degree, I was making a great salary—more than many of my college peers—and it was hard for me to see beyond that. But Bob Seymour really liked me because I was a hard worker (the *Lower Level Success* mentioned in the **Preparation** section), and he saw value in my skill and ability, and he decided to become my sponsor and push me forward. When a position opened in the marketing office that he felt was a good fit for me, he worked on my behalf and he sponsored me to get that position.

Lisa Lutoff-Perlo, CEO of Celebrity Cruises, the first woman CEO ever of a major cruise line, has another story of a male supervisor pushing her toward success beyond what she thought possible. In *Diversity Woman*'s Summer 2016 issue, we highlighted her story of sponsorship. Seventeen years into her career, with aspirations to head her sales department, she was unexpectedly moved to the marketing department by her supervisor, Dan Hanrahan. Lutoff-Perlo was crushed, thinking her career advancement was being stalled, but she later found out that her supervisor, who was also president and CEO of the company, saw her huge potential and wanted to give her an opportunity to learn all parts of the organization. He was being her sponsor and giving her a chance to develop her preparation tools. Lisa rose through the ranks at Celebrity over the next twelve years and eventually became president and CEO in 2014. Looking back, she admitted that prior to being moved to the marketing department by her supervisor and sponsor, she had been aiming low, especially given the potential she exuded as a leader. This is something women in particular struggle with and it hampers their advancement to executive leadership roles. As CEO, Lisa Lutoff-Perlo now has the opportunity to sponsor other women in the organization, a source of great pride for her. She was the one to hire the first female American ship captain of a mega-cruise ship in the U.S. Lisa said of this decision, "I considered it a part of my responsibility to use my opportunity to pay it forward and help not only other women, but other people in a meaningful way."[13]

---

13 Jackie Krentzman, "Even Keel," *Diversity Woman*, Summer 2016, 33.

One of my former customers, Anise Wiley-Little, has another incredible story about the power of having a well-connected advocate. After twenty-seven years in the corporate HR field, Wiley-Little retired from her day job and decided to pursue new interests. But she made the conscious effort to continue to stay connected in her professional network, especially because this type of personal engagement was something she had particularly enjoyed about her former job and career. Years after she left that corporate role, she was contacted by her former sponsor, an executive in the company she had left. He was serving on the board with another leader who was seeking someone to fill an HR and Diversity role at his organization. This former sponsor was able to speak to the quality and impact of her work, which enticed this new prospective employer. Anise said, though, that during those first few conversations with her former sponsor, "I had no idea that he was in the background paving the way and opening the door . . . You never know who in your network will lead you to something unexpected." She was eventually tapped for the role and she is now the Chief Human Capital and Diversity Officer at Northwestern University's Kellogg School of Management where she helps budding executives understand the business value and implementation strategies of diversity and inclusion. What a testament to the power of a strategic network and a well-connected advocate! She kept herself visible and she left a lasting impression on her sponsor even years after he first advocated for her. Wiley-Little said, "Being strategically connected pays off and can come full circle and present opportunities when they are least expected when those relationships are nurtured in the right way." This is an especially important point for underserved groups to remember and utilize—specifically women and people of color. This is why this tool kit for women's leadership success is so important. You don't know who's out there with the right connections so that when a need arises, your name is still on their mind.

TRAINING PROGRAMS

Training programs often focus on general leadership development, teambuilding, or communication skills. Corporations are beginning to institute more training programs that are aimed toward women's advancement as they become more aware of the benefits of gender inclusion. As a woman, you should participate in any leadership training programs available to you so that you can acquire adequate skills and knowledge in leadership and become more competitive on the C-Suite track. These can be programs that offer certifications, professional clubs to help improve your leadership

skills or build your network, or social or educational programs that help you with your **Preparation** tools.

I think it's so important to seek out organizations that
value their human talent. For a long time at Dupont, I worked
for a particular department manager who was one the most
forward-thinking for women at that time. I was never turned
down for training and development, and not only did the
department allow employees to seek out external training
opportunities, they made sure they brought those training
and development opportunities in-house. I even had a supervisor once sponsor me to join Toastmasters so I would be
better prepared to give presentations to the all-male team of
about ten to fifteen engineers and sales executives. Another
time at Dupont, after I had been recently promoted into a
marketing & PR position, I was attending a huge event for
the movie *Chicago* when it was released. I was responsible
for marketing and branding for the hosiery that was used
in the movie. I was at this event doing a promotion in front
of Bloomingdales with the director, and with the star of the
movie, Queen Latifah. Generally, the paparazzi and the press
are at these events and they only want to talk to the celebrities and big time stars. Thus I was not prepared to speak; I
was just there as a representative of my company. Well, the
PR agent hired by Dupont for the event happened to know
one of the backstage reporters from E! Entertainment, and

she came to me and told me she'd already talked to her about putting me on air. Before I could think, there was a microphone in my face . . . and I froze! It was a missed opportunity to promote my company and for the agency to get credit for getting us on camera with top celebrities. But when I got back to work, instead of being penalized for being unprepared, my team treated it as an opportunity for me to become prepared. They valued me and my work, and they understood that I didn't have the proper training. Within two weeks they had spent $10K for me to go through broadcast and on-air training. It was so awesome! I went to New York for two weeks and received on-camera training, and I ended up having a great career in PR with Dupont. A lot of that training I received is what has helped me be successful in what I do today. Never pass an opportunity to attend training programs and advance your skills. This is an invaluable tool to use in your advancement to the C-Suite and it is another way you can begin building your strategic network of relationships.

ESSENTIAL TOOL SET #4

CREATING AN ENGAGING CORPORATE CULTURE

This fourth and last set of tools is a bit different than the other three. The **Executive Traits, Preparation,** and **Building Strategic Relationships** tool sets focus on personal factors that drive individuals to advance. The focus here in the tools for **Creating an Engaging Corporate Culture** is on drivers for advancement within the business itself. The culture of an organization includes the values, beliefs, attitudes, behaviors, and other intangible elements of business that have developed over time and through the interaction of its members. Biases appear in most cultures and include the unspoken understandings within an organization that do not appear on job descriptions or performance reviews. These institutional and cultural biases can have either a positive or negative effect on women's advancement opportunities, depending on the nature of the bias. Generally, though, a company's implicit negative gender bias is one of the biggest barriers to women's advancement. An organizational culture that is (even subconsciously) negative toward women frequently impacts other social factors, such as family-life commitments, and can even ultimately drive away women who have already reached the top. In short, this type of organizational culture obviously works against a woman's ambitions.

Many times a corporate culture values the "masculine" stereotype of leadership that encompasses the characteristics of "independence, internal competition, self-promotion, overt ambitiousness, decisiveness, aggressiveness, as well as the creation of power and status."[1] This can be less welcoming to women than a culture that values "cooperation, harmony, and participation."[2] Skeptics will cast doubt as

---

1   Geert Hofstede, Gert Jan Hofstede, and Michael Minkov, *Cultures and Organizations: Software for the Mind,* 3rd Edition, McGraw-Hill, 576.

2   Hofstede et al., *Cultures and Organizations,* 576.

to the existence of this dominant masculine culture today, and many will argue that most organizational cultures are continuously changing to be more inclusive, especially because technology and globalization are changing the ways we communicate and interface. But we know for a fact that the number of women who reach the C-Suite remains disproportionately low, even though more women have entered the pipeline and, theoretically, should have advanced to that level. Often women are not able to achieve the top rung specifically because of gender bias in the organizational culture that discourages women's advancement beyond a certain management level, particularly if they do not possess the conventional male leadership traits.[3] It's true that advancement programs designed for women, as well as positive changes in organizational culture, such as diversity initiatives and the adoption of inclusive leadership styles, have helped women progress up the corporate ladder—but only so far.

The issue of American women's limited access to the C-Suite has a long and well-documented history. In 1976, *McKinsey Quarterly* director James E. Bennett wrote that businesses looking honestly at the advancement of women in their own organizations would uncover gender bias issues

---

3   Yafang Tsai, "Relationship Between Organizational Culture, Leadership Behavior and Job Satisfaction," *BMC Health Services Research*, May 14, 2011.

despite the feeling among male executives that the women's liberation movement had already solved those issues.[4] Thirty-eight years later, in 2014, another *McKinsey Quarterly* report referred to Bennett's article after surveying another 1,421 global executives and finding that cultural attitudes and gender bias were still key players in the lack of diversity at the corporate level.[5] The survey showed that the gender bias issues flagged by Bennett are long-lived and pervasive. Yet, many other studies cited in this book show that the presence of women at the highest levels of corporations boosts performance and the bottom line! But still, the nagging gender imbalance in the C-Suite shows the "impermeability of the glass ceiling."[6] This also means there's an imbalance in the decision-making abilities of corporations because there's a lack of diversity on boards, in upper management, and in the C-Suite. As a woman who wants to advance in leadership, you must first acknowledge that these biases exist. So first, you need to identify some of these unspoken prejudices and

4   Sandrine Devillard, Sandra Sancier-Sultan, and Charlotte Werner, "Why Gender Diversity at the Top Remains a Challenge," *McKinsey Quarterly*, April 2014, http://www.mckinsey.com/business-functions/organization/our-insights/why-gender-diversity-at-the-top-remains-a-challenge

5   Devillard et al., "Why Gender Diversity at the Top Remains a Challenge."

6   Justin Wolfers, "Fewer Women Run Big Companies than Men Named John," *New York Times*, March 2, 2015, https://www.nytimes.com/2015/03/03/upshot/fewer-women-run-big-companies-than-men-named-john.html?_r=1&abt=0002&abg=1

how they affect your growth potential. Then you can identify how you can use your personal strengths to move beyond these barriers to create an engaging culture. This is a much more effective and self-assertive approach, rather than just focusing on how organizations might need to change in order to accommodate your progress as a woman.

The dynamic and legendary female leader, Joyce Russell, now president of Adecco, spoke at Diversity Woman Media's 2016 national Business Leadership Conference. She stated, that if you are a woman, and you are not moving up in your organization, you are either are in the wrong organization, or you have the wrong boss. The point Russell was making was that, sometimes, no matter how active and assertive you are in your work environment, and no matter how impressive your accomplishments, you may still fail to be properly recognized or promoted. It is important that you use your tools to respond to the situation at hand, even if it means moving to another organization if the existing institutional factors prove too much of a hindrance to your personal advancement. Then you can move on to utilizing your sharpened tools to develop an inclusive and engaging corporate culture within your new organization. It's only then that you can thrive and progress in your career goals.

UNDERSTANDING UNSTATED CRITERIA

Many researchers believe leadership should be based solely on the abilities, skills, and knowledge of the leaders, rather than on social and cultural attitudes and beliefs that might give preference to specifically masculine leadership styles and ways of thinking. These latter elements are the so-called "unstated criteria"—hard enough to pinpoint, let alone meet—and yet form a significant hindrance to women gaining entry into the chief suite. In addition, these intangible requirements for advancement often vary, based on the specific organizational culture.

This set of unstated criteria for promotion—the unwritten requirements and distinct competencies associated with advancement—constitutes one of the greatest obstacles to the advancement of women to the C-Suite. These competencies don't typically appear in a job description or on a performance review, but they have a strong influence on a person's ability to advance. Researchers Beeson and Valerio have developed three general categories to describe them, and these are the unstated criteria you should be focusing on.

▨ The first are **non-negotiables**, including a strong track record, ethics and integrity, and a drive to lead.[7] These mirror the *Education* and *Early Career Success* tools in the **Preparation** tool set, and *Passion* and *Leadership* from the **Executive Traits** tool set. Sharpening these tools will help you meet these non-negotiable criteria.

▨ The second are **de-selection factors**, including weak interpersonal skills, abrasive or insensitive treatment of others, putting one's self-interest above the company's good, and holding a narrow perspective in the business.[8] These would indicate a lack of the *Emotional Intelligence* tool, and possibly the lack of a *Mentoring* or *Sponsoring* tool, for example. Avoid these pitfalls that could prevent your advancement.

▨ The third are **core selection factors**, including strategic skills, building a strong team, managing implementation, initiating innovation and change, lateral management, and executive presence.[9] Here, the

---

7 John Beeson and Anna Marie Valerio, "The Executive Leadership Imperative: A New Perspective on How Companies and Executives Can Accelerate the Development of Women Leaders," *Business Horizons,* September 2012, 417–425.

8 Beeson and Valerio, "The Executive Leadership Imperative," 417–425.

9 "The Executive Leadership Imperative," 417–425.

Building a Network tool from the **Building Strategic Relationships** tool set, and the key **Executive Traits** tools of *Confidence* and *Assertiveness* are essential.

You'll notice that these categories of unstated criteria are gender neutral on the surface. But in practice they present many hurdles for women. First, women are less likely to get effective feedback compared to men, or no direct feedback at all, on these criteria. Additionally, built-in biases can lead others to perceive an exaggerated level of the de-selection factors in women, like a negative perception of assertiveness. Additionally, lack of opportunities, such as "stretch assignments," can keep women from demonstrating the core selection factors. All of the unstated criteria mentioned, whether it's having the "right" traits or not having the "wrong" traits, actually stem from a long history of gender bias and are often inherent in an organization's DNA. Women have to recognize where they fit in on this scale and understand how to adapt their behavior to address these issues within their organization. Again, this is where the application of tools from the other three tool sets is invaluable.

This cultural bias and unstated criteria is not limited to gender, either. It extends to racial, cultural, and socioeconomic backgrounds. For example, studies have shown that if you take two copies of the exact same resume, one with a male name on it and the other with a female name on it, the male name will be contacted much more often than the female. Now, take the same resume and put an African-American name on it, and the number of calls drops even further. Bias unequivocally plays a role every step of the way in getting a job. Fifteen years ago when I was laid off from Dupont, I had a hard time even getting interviews for leadership roles I knew I was qualified for. It didn't matter that one of the CEOs still at Dupont, a white male, was acting as a reference and advocating for me within my network. I was up against too much inherent gender, racial, and cultural bias. At that time, I was living in the south, in North Carolina, and looking for leadership opportunities in the manufacturing industry. I continued to prepare and network and finally got an interview with another large manufacturing organization for a senior level marketing manager position. I had four rounds of interviews and every time I came away with stellar reviews. My first interview was with the VP of Human Resources, a black female. My second interview was with her boss in the HR department, a white female. To me, this was a good sign to have such gender diversity at top levels in the industry. The third round interview was with three more VPs within the company, all white males. But still, these men all seemed to think I'd be great at the job. And I was impressed that they were willing to step outside the box of gender and racial bias and could see that I was well qualified and had exactly the kind of experience they needed. So why wouldn't they want to hire me? This was a very high level position I was trying for, so the final round interview was with the CEO of the company. I got myself prepared. I checked everything off the list—my appearance was professional and well groomed, I practiced interviewing and I was on top of my game. I knew that if I didn't get this position, it wouldn't be because I wasn't prepared; it would have to be because of some other bias within the organization.

When I walked into the interview and saw a young white male, I thought to myself, "Great! He's my age, he's a baby boomer, and he's got to be an innovative, forward-thinking guy. He's going to find real value in all of this marketing experience and background I have." And he did! His words to me were, "Sheila, you have more brand experience than we could ever even need and I commend you on that." But then he said, "But I am afraid that you are not the right fit." What he meant was that I wasn't a fit for the organization or the department. This was a consumer packaging/manufacturing company and I would have had approximately thirty men, predominately white, reporting to me for marketing. The CEO was uneasy that this pool of his workforce would not accept me in this leadership role, and he was concerned about having disgruntled employees and losing productivity.

This harks back to Joyce Russell's comment mentioned earlier. The problem wasn't me; rather it was the organization. Maybe it was even the wrong industry. When the president of that company told me I wasn't the right fit, it was then that I realized I would constantly be spinning my wheels and was not going to advance on the path I was on. At the time, I was married and living in North Carolina. I knew relocation wasn't an option, but it was also unlikely that I would ever get the same career opportunities in another leadership role, like I had at Dupont, with a similar company. I was just going to be continually discriminated against when trying for the type of leadership roles I was clearly so qualified for.

This is when I first decided to explore my vision to start my magazine. I wanted to help other women overcome these same challenges and adversities, and provide them with ideas, solutions, and resources to advance in their career. In fact, the first column in the first edition of my national magazine was entitled "The Right Fit." I had started investigating this phenomenon or trend where organizations asserted that a candidate had to be the "right fit" in order to be hired. What did that mean and how could that be used to discriminate against women and people of color? It was a real turning point in my career path and was a direct result of being able to identify these unstated criteria and cultural biases and developing tools to overcome those barriers to advancement. Now my career has reached heights I never could have imagined had I tried to pursue a leadership role in the manufacturing industry in the south.

RECOGNIZING UNCONSCIOUS GENDER BIAS

Literature on the relationship between corporate culture and women's advancement describes bias as thought patterns, assumptions, and interpretations based on beliefs usually learned at an early age, or from others who are looked up to.[10] These assumptions, whether positive or negative, are often ingrained and inflexible.[11] Going a step further, Howard J. Ross, in his book *Everyday Bias: Identifying and Navigating Unconscious Judgments in Our Daily Lives*, identifies "unconscious bias" as a "tendency or inclination that results in judgment without question."[12] Unconscious bias occurs without awareness, intention, or knowledge. Two

---

10 Trang Chu, "How Unconscious Bias Holds Us Back," *The Guardian*, May 1, 2014, http://www.theguardian.com/women-in-leadership/2014/may/01/unconscious-bias-women-holding-back-work

11 Sahar Andrade, "Workplace Diversity: What is Unconscious Bias & How to Manage It?" *LinkedIn*, June 18, 2014, https://www.linkedin.com/pulse/20140618145805-35065017-workplace-diversity-what-is-unconscious-bias-how-to-manage-it

12 Howard J. Ross, *Everyday Bias: Identifying and Navigating Unconscious Judgments in Our Daily Lives*, Rowman & Littlefield, 2014.

thirds of the executives I interviewed during my dissertation research mentioned unconscious biases as a factor in women's advancement to the C-Suite. Some pointed out that overt biases, like what I faced when I was interviewing in predominately white male manufacturing organizations two decades ago, are less common than they were in the past, but unconscious biases (or unwritten expectations) are still a frequent deterrent to progress.

As we've learned, women also typically have a different leadership style than men, which can create additional deep-rooted gender biases in organizations. Women are generally better collaborators and better team builders. They often have greater emotional intelligence and are better at building those strategic relationships. But in the **Executive Traits** section, I mentioned that there has been a presumptive "male" style of leadership necessary for actually advancing to the C-Suite. This male leadership style includes traits like being aggressive, transactional, results-oriented, and focused on positional power, whereas the traditional female leadership style involves traits that are more "relational" and people-focused. This disparity in styles is causing women to lag behind on the corporate ladder. Deborah Tannen, who I referred to when discussing the *Assertiveness* tool, relates these gender-based differences back to early social development of girls and boys.[13] Girls look for ways to communicate and relate with each other and they avoid being bossy to each other. As adults, women continue to focus on closeness, while men continue to focus on status. Men are likely to be more direct, while women are more likely to make indirect suggestions. Men tease each other with play insults, while women connect to each other with compliments. Women are more likely to build rapport by talking about their problems, their family, and their home, while men are more likely to talk about their hobbies, with a focus on the details and statistics. But this translates into that "double-bind" for them once they enter the workplace. In corporate America, women have historically been expected to take on a male-dominant style to advance to the C-Suite while somehow still maintaining their feminine nature—an inherent contradiction. Thus this unspoken expectation that members of the C-Suite should have the leadership characteristics of a typical male leader becomes a gender bias for women seeking to advance to the top. What's interesting is that other research conducted by Susan Eisner shows that at least 85 percent of corporate executives queried, both male and female, exhibited leadership traits that were *both* "positional" and "personal."[14] Further research

13 Deborah Tannen, *Talking from 9 to 5*.

14 Susan Eisner, "Leadership: Gender and Executive Style," *SAM Advanced Management Journal*, January 2013, 26–41.

showed that leaders who did exhibit the more traditional female styles, like being team-based and consensus-driven, actually helped leaders (both men and women) be even more effective.[15] But in spite of the hard statistics, this assumption about the necessity of the male leadership style persists, and until we can eliminate these stereotypes and hire women based on their unique qualifications instead of trying to find and hire women who lead like a man, women will not progress to the same higher positions as their male colleagues. The good news is that leaders are finally becoming aware of just how big the gap is between the perception of traits required to be an effective leader versus the actual traits of leaders that rise to the top.

The Summer 2014 issue of *Diversity Woman* contained an article titled "Men as Allies," which featured several male executives dedicated to achieving gender diversity and equality in their organizations. In the article, we introduced the concept of "micro-inequities." Those are subtle but cumulative messages that promote a negative bias and demoralize women and other under-represented groups. Examples of these micro-inequities might be checking emails or texting

---

15 Steven H. Appelbaum, Lynda Audet, and Joanne C. Miller, "Gender and Leadership? Leadership and Gender? A Journey Through the Landscape of Theories," *Leadership & Organization Development Journal*, Volume 24, Issue 1, 43–51.

during a face-to-face conversation with a woman, interrupting mid-sentence, or making eye contact only with men when talking to a group of both genders. It's often an unconscious behavior but it disrespects women. Steve Pemberton, Divisional Vice President & Chief Diversity Officer for Walgreens, said he has done micro-inequality training for his employees. He said, "It's important to know that the culture in which we live brings certain biases, that if you don't have armor on, you may be a known participant, hence promoting micro-inequalities. You may not even know that every time a woman talks, you don't give her your full attention. Combating micro-inequalities is a matter of awareness and education."[16] Reginald Van Lee, Executive Vice President at Booz Allen Hamilton stated, "It's on all of us. From the senior leadership to the managers and down, we are responsible for making sure there is an inviting environment for not just women, but for all groups."[17] This starts with formal training programs like what Pemberton has initiated at Walgreens, and also includes deliberate mentoring and advocating from male counterparts.

I've already mentioned my early years in the manufacturing division at Dupont and that I had an exceptional

---

16 Jackie Krentzman, "Men as Allies," *Diversity Woman,* Summer 2014, 33.

17 Krentzman, "Men as Allies," 31.

supervisor Mr. Bob Seymour, who was my sponsor in every way. But I didn't always have a supportive and open-minded leader. When I first moved over into the marketing department as an administrative assistant in 1990, my first boss was not supportive at all. It was rumored that he held others back—even other white male colleagues. He made it clear that I would not get a promotion in his department and told me there was no room for advancement. It was clear I had the wrong boss who had created a bad culture. I was getting ready to just quit when Bob Francois came in as a new manager and started to fix things. From the beginning he found value in my work performance. He gave me all kinds of opportunities to explore the marketing department, and as he got to know me, he developed a new role just for me as a marketing/communications representative. He started reorganizing the entire department, which allowed me room for advancement. It's interesting how even one person can affect enough change to bring down barriers, especially those of unconscious gender and cultural biases within an organization. Bob Francois did just that—he created an engaging culture.

OVERCOMING BIAS & CREATING AN ENGAGING CORPORATE CULTURE

As women, we must act as shepherds to bring in a more engaging corporate culture for all members of the organization. The findings from my research, and much of the research on unconscious bias and unwritten expectations shows that women who have made it to the C-Suite chose not to see those negatives as barriers but as fact-of-life challenges to work through. This is the same mindset necessary to develop the *Life Choices* tool in the **Preparation** tool set. Because these successful women cultivated executive traits such as confidence, courage, and assertiveness and exhibited leadership skills, they were able to reach their goals. Fortunately, society has at last begun to make the shift toward more gender equality, from a broader shift to work-life balance for both males and females, to gender-neutral training and mentorship programs. However, an unstated bias still persists in many corporate cultures today. We as women need to understand that these biases exist and at the times we meet these barriers we must be prepared to use all of our **Executive Traits** tools to adapt to and also change the environment. We must engage the organizational culture in a different and effective way. Hard work and "small wins," relationship building, effective communication, and risk-taking are all imperative for women to overcome these gender biases and stereotypes and to re-define the culture.

It's also important to make the decision early on in your career about whether the organization you are working for is a good cultural fit for your advancement goals and whether it is in your best interest to remain there. This perspective suggests a shift in approach from "I need this company" to "this company needs me." You have the skill, the talent, the experience, and the confidence to excel in the role you're aspiring to, and you need to have the courage and willingness to find another company when the values and goals do not align with your own. We need a culture of equality across corporate America and it starts with having focused, assertive, confident women making their way up the leadership ladder.

It was because I exhibited the executive traits of leadership, visibility, confidence, and courage in my position at Dupont that Bob Seymour was able to see my potential and help me to make the leap from a manufacturing to a marketing role. But when I made that leap over to this new role, I was in a new context that had a totally new and different organizational culture that I had to learn how to navigate through. At that time at Dupont, the R&D department staff were predominately white males in engineering and business development roles. In addition, the entire team was responsible for their own marketing and communications budget. But when my new manager, Bob Francois, created my new position and promoted me to Marketing/Communications Representative, the team lost that autonomy and now they had to come to me and ask for sales kits, ad space, and so on. I now had the power to control the budget; I assessed the needs, and I had approval rights. Culturally this was a huge disruption to what the department was accustomed to, not only because of the change in the way they had been conducting business, but also because they now had a woman of color as the decision maker holding the purse strings. This was a great challenge for the team and for me. A great leader is able to influence change in a positive way, and my manager had created an engaging organizational culture that allowed a much smoother path for me to be successful in this role and also allowed my colleagues to step outside their comfort zone and trust me. I positioned myself as leader and I took the job and my performance seriously. I utilized my executive traits of *Confidence, Assertiveness, Leadership,* and *Emotional Intelligence.* I was so passionate about my work and this great opportunity I had been given, and I strategized and looked for any opportunity for us all to collaborate. The team members began to see that having me manage their marketing budget actually made their world a whole lot easier. They started to seek me out for my opinions in marketing meetings and began to see me as thought leader. They also trusted me because I produced results. In other words, I had *Early Career Success* and was developing my *Broad Business Learning*. What's more, I had a phenomenal manager who was a mentor, coach, and a sponsor. So even though this was one of the most challenging times in my career, particularly because of gender and cultural bias, I realize today that the same tools that came out of my research are actually what I exhibited over my career and are what allowed me to get ahead.

As a woman developing your unique leadership traits to make it to the C-Suite, you need to be aware of the corporate culture you're working within, and you need to identify and understand the unstated criteria for getting ahead and the unconscious bias that may create hurdles along your path. Don't just rely on what's written in your job description or in your performance review for clues on what criteria will be used to judge your advancement potential. You must exercise your tools of emotional intelligence and be perceptive to the unspoken expectations. Only then will you have a clear sightline and be able to plot a clearer path to the C-Suite.

The big picture is that excluding women and other diverse groups from executive positions means businesses are failing to take full advantage of the skills and abilities of a large portion of the workforce. Women make up half of the workforce and bring their own unique set of executive traits, experience and preparation tools, and strategic networks of relationships that are being left untapped. This isn't just a cultural problem, it's an economic problem. The general business benefits of including women in a company structure are already widely documented but have been slow to be adopted in many organizations. When speaking about the need for gender equality, Steve Pemberton in the "Men As Allies" article said, ". . . this is about the health of the company." Reginald Van Lee reiterated that notion: "An organization with diversity of opinions and perspectives is a healthy one."[18]

Finally, as you do advance, make sure you clear the way for more women to follow in your footsteps. Like all tools in your tool kit, it works two ways. You have to be as open to giving as you are to receiving. This not only develops greater gender diversity in the workplace but it allows you an opportunity to engage and affect positive change within your own organizational cultures.

---

18 "Men as Allies," 30–31.

CONCLUSION

As stated in the Introduction, I have dedicated my own professional career to empowering women in their quest for advancement, and it is my mission as a thought leader to share these ideas and insights that I've gained through my research and years of experience. I developed these four sets of essential tools discussed in this book because I believe they are key to helping women break through the glass ceiling so that only the sky is the limit when it comes to their professional career advancement.

Remember, these tools do not stand alone. They are interrelated and interdependent on each other, and a successful combination of all of these elements is what will help women succeed at the corporate level. For example, general work relationships can develop into strong networks where a woman might find mentors, and mentors could eventually become sponsors. Furthermore, a lack of strength in one factor can sometimes offset another. For example, hard work and experience can sometimes substitute for formal education for a woman who has made a life choice that prioritizes time with her children over acquiring an MBA. Likewise, each set of tools in the tool kit relates to the other sets in mutually supportive ways. For example, an executive trait such as confidence can play a large part in a woman's ability to build personal and professional connections, and those connections in turn will boost her confidence. Confidence and networking can also support life choices and equip a woman to deal with challenges in the corporate culture. These combinations can both trigger and foster an upward cycle of accumulating and accelerating success towards ultimate advancement into the C-Suite. Let's review again the four sets of essential tools in our Tool Kit for Success.

ESSENTIAL TOOL SET #1:
EXECUTIVE TRAITS

Your internal motivation, optimism, and self-empowerment

- Confidence
- Assertiveness
- Courage
- Passion
- Visibility
- Leadership
- Emotional Intelligence

ESSENTIAL TOOL SET #2:
PREPARATION

Your strategic initiatives to position yourself for advancement

- Life Choices
- Education
- Early Career Success
- Broad Business Learning

ESSENTIAL TOOL SET #3:
BUILDING STRATEGIC RELATIONSHIPS

Your personal and professional connections

- Building a Network
- Mentoring
- Coaching
- Sponsoring
- Training Programs

ESSENTIAL TOOL SET #4:
CREATING AN ENGAGING
CORPORATE CULTURE

Your awareness and appropriate response to the tacit understandings and biases that hinder women and minorities

- Understanding Unstated Criteria
- Recognizing Unconscious Gender Bias
- Overcoming Bias & Creating an Engaging Corporate Culture

We know that the advancement of women in corporate America today is problematic, but my focus in this book has been on solutions. I've shared some of the tips, strategies, and stories that so many other successful men and women have used to advance to the C-Suite before us. Those women certainly encountered many of these barriers I've talked about in this book, like gender, racial, and cultural bias. But they chose to see them as challenges to work through, rather than as uncontrollable negative forces. The agent of advancement for these women was the woman herself—the way that she combined, controlled, and in some cases created the factors that propelled her to the C-Suite.

I hope you have found inspiration and motivation from reading this book and can take this research as a guide along with you as you advance in your career—because the fundamental thing to remember is that this is about continuous learning and improvement. It's about understanding which tools fit you best and applying that understanding to your own life. It's not about picking up the tool once and then putting it back in the tool box to rust. You can begin to employ and benefit from these strategies at any stage in your career and continue to develop them until you've reached the highest levels to which you aspire.

Stay the course, and I'll see you at the top!

ABOUT THE AUTHOR

Dr. Sheila Robinson is the Founder and Publisher of *Diversity Woman Magazine*, a professional business magazine for women leaders, executives and entrepreneurs of all races, cultures and backgrounds. Robinson began publishing in 2005 with the launch of the North Carolina Career Network, and due to an overwhelming national response to its success, the publication expanded nationally in 2008, becoming *Diversity Woman*. Robinson has dedicated her life to providing women ideas, solutions and resources to help them advance and reach their professional goals.

Dr. Robinson's background includes over twenty years in corporate America including her last role as a former Marketing Director in DuPont's global textiles division, in which she was responsible for all marketing communications, public relations and brand development functions for its Lycra®

apparel business, including advertising, media relations, crisis management, retail promotions, and trend and sales presentations.

She holds certificates from Stanford University's Professional Publishing Program (2007) and Wharton's School of Business Chief Learning Officer Program (2013).

She holds a bachelor's degree in Pre-Law from North Carolina Central University, and two master's degrees: Master of Entrepreneurship & Innovation, with Honors, from Western Carolina University; and Master of Science in Education from the University of Pennsylvania. In 2016, she earned a Chief Learning Officer Doctorate of Education in Talent Management from The University of Pennsylvania.

She is the author of *Lead by Example: An Insiders Look At How To Successfully Lead in Corporate America and Entrepreneurship* (2014), which has an accompanying workbook.

In 2009, Robinson was featured on the cover of *Publishing Executive* Magazine's list of 50 Top Women in Magazine Publishing for the significant contribution she has made in her industry.

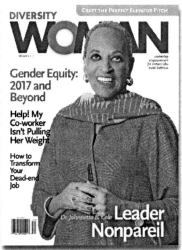

CPSIA information can be obtained
at www.ICGtesting.com
Printed in the USA
FFOW05n0131060517